Out of the Storm

A Story of PTSD in the Life of a Paramedic

Out of the Storm

A Story of PTSD in the Life of a Paramedic

G. F. Connors

Out of the Storm

A Story of PTSD in the Life of a Paramedic

G. F. Connors

First Print Edition June 2021

Copyright © 2021 G. F. Connors

ISBN: 978-1-989346-28-0

This memoir is a truthful recollection of actual events in the author's life. Some conversations have been recreated and/or supplemented. Names of places have been changed for the sake of privacy. The names and details of some individuals have been changed to respect their privacy.

All rights reserved. No part of this book may be reproduced in any form or by electronic or mechanical means – except in the case of brief quotations embodied in articles or reviews – without written permission of the author or publisher.

New Dawning Press is committed to integrity and publishing quality books. In that spirit, we are pleased to offer this book. However, the story and the words are the author's alone.

DEDICATION

Composing this book over the past three years has been a challenge I hadn't expected to be in until I found myself right in the thick of it. I thought of my family often during the midst of writing and with that in mind, I would like to dedicate this book to the six of them. Over the years, they heard of my writing now and again and they were the ones who would silently support me, all without knowingly being a participant in that role.

This is also dedicated to paramedics everywhere.

PREFACE

The working period in my life amounts to just less than fifty years. Fifty years of having maintained a suitable form of work to earn what I considered a substantial wage, beginning with decent, part-time jobs in the early 1970's. Driving truck while delivering building/construction materials, hotel/food industry while bartending, serving, deliveries, convention set-ups in hotels, landscaping, factory work, community service while life-guarding/instruction, Brewer's Retail deliveries and sales. (Young-uns will need to research that last one!)

In my early 20's, when I began in the ambulance business, I had maybe ten years of work experience behind me. But what I was able to bring to the table was eight or ten different lines of work history, in which each and every one brought along their own unique selection of learning and life experiences. I was still wet enough behind the ears that the possibility of becoming injured on the job was still a distant concern for me but, due to the nature and mechanics of our work in EMS, muscular/joint issues seemed to be the norm. I can surmise that employee turnover was also just as typical fifty or sixty years ago; a practice which would continue through the decades up until today. As in my case, those of us who had chosen to remain in the field had already been introduced to the rapid pace of ambulance work and the various emotional pitches that accompanied select events that were encountered while performing our duties.

It remains doubtful that everyone in this industry can sidestep becoming affected by these emotionally traumatizing events, at least in some way. With professional assistance during my own career, I was able to have a definitive pattern of PTSD symptoms pointed out to me. Up front in the ambulance business, it appeared there was very little being done to address this issue and assist those who were affected. Behind the scenes, it was the same. Not all agencies were acknowledging and tackling the issue of PTSD head-on, not by any means.

I decided not to include in this book, the treatments for PTSD, as obviously, there are plenty of reference materials available. My own symptoms were present years ago, and were later recognized to be PTSD relevant. Yet, prior to them being identified, I understood and considered these symptoms to be signs of other issues, including depression, anxiety, alcohol abuse, and relationship concerns, to name just a few.

This writing identifies my own unique way of plodding through life, only to realize that I am not alone, but indeed part of a group of others who are experiencing very similar circumstances but may not have been able to recognize what is actually going on. Being able to tell my own story, which is so very private and personal, was something I managed to overcome. However, having to document several disturbing components for the book forced me to relive various experiences, which initially caught me off guard and demanded that I periodically step away from writing until I was able to restart with a clearer head. It's kind of difficult to explain, but as you read along, I'm sure all will become much clearer.

INTRODUCTION

While working in one of the management positions I held throughout my career, writing policies or memorandums was sometimes part of my responsibilities. Anyone who has shared a similar position can attest, some days the ideas will flow so readily they were almost difficult to keep up with. The next day while working on the same assignment, I couldn't string a short sentence together to form a thought.

Shortly after leaving my EMS position, I began documenting my days in a journal format which eventually transitioned into what you're reading now. Several efforts to get this writing underway were frequently met with speed bumps or total blockages. And, once I eventually found my groove in late 2018, I still wasn't able to make decent progress until realizing I was only capable of transferring my thoughts onto paper, bypassing the computer keyboard altogether. I knew it made more sense to do the opposite, thus eliminating the transfer of content from paper to laptop but, old habits do die hard, and being near sixty years old at the time, the majority of writing I had done in life was accomplished using pen and paper, rarely on a keyboard.

With notepads and pens, I slipped on my specs (my Ben Franklin's) and took off, pen to paper, burning through the supplies. It began slowly, but once the ideas snowballed and found their attachment, off it went. That said, three or four weeks of generous writing could quickly fizzle out to a dead stop. The triggers I stirred up while documenting and reliving disturbing moments would sideline my efforts, sometimes for weeks or even a couple months. Eventually, after returning from a few of these unplanned breaks, I found the transfer from paper to laptop wasn't near as bad. After my mind eventually surrendered, I was able to tap away on the keys, placing pen and paper aside, and continue with my story. Throughout the next three years, these flashbacks and issues would rear their ugly heads now and then, but thankfully less frequently as in the beginning.

My name is G and I am someone who takes pride in my family, my work, and many other achievements in my life. My career was in EMS, as a Primary Care Paramedic (PCP). I am sincerely indebted to those who have guided and assisted me, especially of late while dealing with my ongoing journey. I have been diagnosed with Complex PTSD, a condition brought on from events experienced throughout my EMS career and early life.

For most of my adult life I have been in the business of helping those in need. Although I am no longer able to return to my career, I will always remain at heart, a medic. For many of us, it's once a medic, always a medic. My career was my passion and with the passing of time, I eventually learned and accepted the fact, those years were an amazing ride. As difficult as it was to leave, it was time to move on from all aspects of EMS.

November 11th, Remembrance Day. For the past few years, I have followed the stories of Canadians who had fought overseas to defeat the evil of those who also fought valiantly to overcome and defeat the good as we know today. We all cringe to think how vastly different our lives could be right now, had the evil regime prevailed in the outcome of WWII. Every fall season, several stories are profiled to mark the anniversary of the end of the war, illustrating those who survived and others who perished during the war, and at what cost. The episodes would feature men and women recounting the roles they played during this period, providing us glimpses into the savage brutality and the horrific events they witnessed or were a part of. They lived through this time of unparalleled history. A few of these episodes stuck with me, becoming solid reminders.

WWI came to an end just over 100 years ago. WWII ended seventy-five years ago, and, in my opinion, this number is also slowly crowding the one century mark.
These battle-hardened men and women who fought throughout Europe, who are portrayed in these short stories were nothing short of heroic and courageous. Here we are in the year 2021 and with all

due respect, when referring to PTSD, have we honestly come leaps and bounds with advances in the treatments of shell-shock and battle fatigue from decades earlier?

Some of the comments from the veterans were as interesting as they were disheartening. One veteran upon returning home to Canada after WWII, said, "You're just like a boiling egg and nobody looks after you." Another went on to say the war didn't end once he arrived back home in Canada, mostly because of the emotional baggage he brought back with him from Europe and subsequently carried throughout his life. From what I understand through his story, he did not receive treatment of any regard and has lived his life the best he could, every day, even with all the symptoms.

In present day, when we look at paramedics who are psychologically affected after their time in the field, they may feel like a boiling egg themselves. The reality is that they require professionally directed and (enhanced) ongoing training on how to manage and bring about continued awareness of their condition. The sad comments of these veterans can mirror the plight of paramedics today. I know this first-hand as eventually I was able to recognize it was the kind of baggage I was also lugging around.

For some paramedics, the number of traumatic injuries and deaths they experience in a period as short as one month is greater than what non-first responder roles will see in a lifetime. And, with all the traumatic experiences, the psychological fallout follows right along with them.

Disclaimer:

With these brief examples, I am in no context comparing the lives of our soldiers in war zones, past or present, with the lives of current paramedics in first world countries. Many psychological injuries can be fueled by traumatic experiences and result in shock, suicide, horrific nightmares, intense anxieties and depression, regardless of the cause.

This writing reflects my own experiences. References to personnel within frontline emergency services may be for example purposes only. This writing does not offer, suggest or recommend therapies or treatments for psychological illnesses indicated. This is my story, it is not intended for purposes of treatment, and the treatments indicated may not be suitable for others.

Within this writing there are several events, descriptions and sensitive situations which have been identified to possibly cause emotional triggers to some readers, regardless whether they are part of the medical field or otherwise.

Please note that several names and identifying references in this composition have been changed to protect the privacy of the individuals involved.

I hope you enjoy my writing.

CHAPTER ONE

When you come out of the storm, you won't be the same person who walked in. That's what this storm is all about. ~ Haruki Murakami

When I encountered my first instances of self-destruction, I found myself away from my own safety area. My safe area was while I was on shift, working within my role as an EMS Primary Care Paramedic (PCP), performing ambulance calls along with dozens of coworkers. Several of these people aren't just coworkers, they're also my colleagues, friends, closer friends, my brothers and sisters.

The images I encountered off-shift, were definitely becoming more common-place than what would be considered 'normal', which forced me to take a step back and ask what this was all about. Often, it would occur while I was parked safely, alone in my car, with the sudden realization that I was in a frozen state, totally numb, my hands on the steering wheel and my mind essentially blank. With help from my therapist, I learned these difficult and uncomfortable episodes of mentally numb experiences are a common trait with those affected with Post Traumatic Stress Disorder, PTSD.

Writing had always been a consideration and I knew in order to be able to document any challenging topic, I wouldn't require volumes of material to make a start. Why not simply talk about a base subject which I think others would find an interest in reading? A subject that I was familiar with, I would enjoy writing about and many could possibly benefit from. Thinking of the thousands of ambulance calls completed by just as many paramedics, the next call never being the same as the last, I thought, *Why not? It's a decent place to begin*. However, the content wouldn't dive into the countless categories of calls within our ambulance work, but instead, it would follow the vastly uncharted direction of the aftermath of our calls. The calls ranged in seriousness; from tough and complicated to no-brainer calls. The tough, complicated and tragic ones had results and consequences that you sometimes couldn't shake. For those unfamiliar with the works of the paramedic field, I have a few examples, written as briefly as possible to offer explanation.

The majority of paramedics maintain a vocabulary familiar to Samuel Jackson, with his potty mouth at its finest.

After each patient contact call and even non-patient contact runs, reports are written, as is standard MOH policy. An example of a non-patient call: a 911 call is received by a Central Ambulance Communications Centre (CACC) when someone has spotted a car accident and is reporting it, not knowing if there is anyone injured. An EMS unit is selected and dispatched to the specific location with details describing said vehicle. The vehicle is located yet there is no one inside or in the general vicinity. Such a scenario could occur many times during a snowstorm when a vehicle may have slid off the roadway and occupants of the vehicle are no longer at the scene, having found or arranged for alternate transportation (meaning they are uninjured). The area would be checked with no one located and a report is completed. The completed report acknowledges the call was received by 911. An ambulance was assigned and had responded, which remains as evidence in the event something actually becomes of the incident. Same steps occur when someone has supposedly been injured in another manner. EMS attends and the patient refuses transport to hospital: a signature of the patient (who refuses treatment and/or transport to a hospital) would be obtained and the crew completes a report, having not transported the patient.

On a 911 call where there is a patient involved, the call taker (the person who actually answers the 911 line) will ask the caller several relevant questions regarding the patient's precise location as well as questions regarding the condition of the patient.

Now, as soon as the call taker has received vital pieces of information, such as the patient's location and they have established a priority of the emergency, this information is electronically sent, in real time, to a dispatcher. The dispatcher selects the closest ambulance station and assigns a crew to the call, providing the crew an address as well as the nature of the call. During the period when the dispatcher received the call information, the call taker has remained on the line with the caller obtaining additional patient (condition) information as well as specifics where the patient can be found if not at a specific address (at the beach, in dense woods, etc). This information is passed to the dispatcher who updates the responding crew. This all happens in real time, generally with no delays.

Many of us are old school and still refer to a report as being written because that's the form of report many of us started with, pen to paper or even pencil to paper and guess what, it had to be, it just had to be an HB brand of pencil. The Ministry of Health, MOH, was, and still is so damn finicky. Too funny, said no seasoned medic ever.

After the call is completed and if we hadn't been dispatched on another one, we'd hang out in our report room in the emergency department or outside while restocking our bags. Cleaning up for the next one, hanging out, simple meaningly chats and ribbing someone. And yup, there's always, always, just one more call.

It was all about the camaraderie here, well, sometimes anyway. (Even though some remain hard-nosed, everyone has at least one soft spot.) We've all dealt with the never-ending death and disease so it's comforting to have someone close by with whom there's an understanding of mutual trust and support. Meaningless chats may occur but many of us maintain that 'on guard' position. Always on alert mentally, always in a protection mode.

So, if you have created an image of our business you're pretty much on board: an EMS crew responds to an address, accesses the patient and provides all necessary treatments. Once the patient is on their way to the hospital in the ambulance, the crew updates the emergency department with information on what they can expect, transfer of care of the patient to emerge staff takes place then finally, the paramedic provides the attending physician a report on the patient. This scenario can be repeated several times per shift, then before we know it we are out the door and on our way home.

This is where my safety zone would end. The completion of our shift was where I would regrettably remove my own game face. I could spot my happy place, the place I felt safest, now distant in the rear-view mirror while leaving the station, heading for home.

PTSD and the term stigma are frequently paired together but in no way do they belong together. Stigma is defined as 'takes away from one's character or reputation'. There are many who may well be affected with PTSD but refuse to report it. Reporting a disturbing call/incident to a supervisor and thus creating a paper trail, could instil a fear of being looked down upon, possibly as a weak medic, as not being tough enough for the work, an outcast. The ones looking down at the others can exhibit negative attitudes and beliefs, thus creating the stigma. More disturbing, there are some who firmly believe (even in 2021) that there is a potential of being released from their position if they report these kinds of calls. Very surprising but yup, I've heard it myself!
This reflects the incidences of intimidation from other paramedics, management, gross misunderstandings on behalf of the paramedics and those in leadership roles. I have been a witness to all of the above. To me, this obviously indicates there are some who would rather just not have to think about a situation or report it, then hide their head in the sand and go on with their own lives, oblivious to the mental damage that could inevitably, slowly and surely, settle in. One does not require a confrontational personality to ensure their views are heard and understood. One just needs to stand up for what they believe is right for themselves and for others who are unable to speak for themselves. A quick bit of research, referring to

the rights of those affected and what is expected of paramedics and management alike, would provide a ton of information and eliminate so many perceived inaccuracies and anxieties.

When it came down to my own mental health, I didn't care what others thought as this struggle was all about me and what I was dealing with in the moment. I've heard the rude and insensitive comments and there will always be someone around to quietly ridicule us. My guess is they don't honestly understand what it is they're being so defensive about. Still, I was able to observe others who initially appeared to be interested, comfortable and supportive yet sadly, given time, they too, proved to be the opposite. Talk about being two-faced!

At the time, research had been completed by a select member of the management of our service, yet nothing had even been placed into a 'file for consideration' until years later. Why bother to do the research, obtain the facts and recognize the consequences of PTSD in EMS, then do nothing about it?

CHAPTER TWO

You simply cannot heal in the environment which made you sick.

I wasn't sure on the direction I should consider once I decided it was in my best interest to leave my profession, a calling I had been ever so passionate about. Months earlier, Lorraine Wilson (my therapist) and I had included this subject in one of our sessions. She was supportive, but it was I who needed to figure out when and how to put all this together, so it would make sense. We talked about it, but she wouldn't tell me how to go about planning my exit.

In our work with EMS, we train, we practice, we prepare so when called upon, everything is so second nature we simply fall into the role. Similarly, as I had been part of this career for so many years, I thought I had planned for and included everything I needed to be aware of. I figured I was able to see the entire picture from where I was. Once I left the station after my final twelve-hour day, what was my next step?

There were also other questions which needed answers. Where would I go and what would I do when the time came to leave, as EMS was essentially all I knew? (Or all that I had ever wanted to know.) This is how scattered I felt while outside of my safe zone, and it turned out that I was more deeply affected than I realized.

My mental health had become an increasing issue for over two years now and my body had been taking a brutal kicking for the past ten, at times forcing extended periods away from work due to these injuries. My head issues were the priority but the physical stresses I experienced were coming in a close second and had begun to form their own potential, career-ending demands.

All aspects of work in the paramedic field relate to triaging and prioritizing, and my current situation wasn't much different. I had been attending regular therapy sessions since 2016 and it was becoming clear that my symptoms of depression, my anxieties and suicidal ideations were all on the increase. It is extremely difficult to treat a patient while they remain in the very situation which is the cause and contributor to their debilitated condition. All evidence indicated I had only a few options available, but just one option was the right one for me. For a brief time, I considered working my way into a job share position or dropping into a part-time role, which would reduce my time being on the road by about half. Our service covered a large geographical area which included twelve EMS stations that were scattered throughout two counties, and serviced both rural and urban populations. That said, once in the part-time pool, the last thing I wanted was to be driving over an hour each way (in ideal weather) to an outlying station.

By the time I had begun this writing, I had spent two years in therapy, accompanied by months of attempting to have my disability claim approved, all while dealing with various professionals in their own fields of expertise. One of these professionals was hands-down, simply amazing, intelligent and considered an expert in her field. Another appeared to be more of a hindrance of sorts to my progression once I decided to leave my career. The third was unable to assist me because of their own (alleged) serious personal or professional issues. Then there was the one who held all the cards; she was following all the rules while in the role of a WSIB case worker, but for me, she created another whole set of challenges. This short story outlines my journey which would take just shy of three months to complete.

Police and fire services have been a part of our history for well over one hundred years, and these services have evolved from a basic and simple idea of protection to the modern, sophisticated, science-based services we are familiar with today.

The ambulance business in Ontario, pre-1970's, was a proud industry and included a dedicated group of men and women whose services were commonly operated out of funeral homes, furniture stores or other businesses at the time. When a call was received, if the ambulance person was unable to find someone (anyone, not always a person connected with the service) to accompany them on the run, they would attend on his or her own. I've been told by some of the seasoned ambulance guys that the training provided was sparse, aside from the required first aid certification.

At some point in the 70's, when they became 100% funded by the province, these ambulance services were privately operated, hospital-based or provincially run. The first community college course offered for ambulance training was held in Borden, Ontario. Known as ambulance attendants at the time, they were taught plenty of procedures which, unfortunately, were not able to be put into practice for many years. Now that, my friends, is a bona fide group of keeners!

Select community colleges in Ontario began offering the Ambulance and Emergency Care Program (AEC) in the late 1970's. The graduates were very well educated with the science skills of EMS, yet were provided a (somewhat) limited selection of equipment with which to do the job, in reference to the education provided. One example being: during my own AEC program of '81/'82, there was more than one emergency room doctor in two of our hospital placements who found it difficult to understand why, while enrolled in the Ontario College programs for ambulance, we were not also receiving training in IV therapy and advanced airway management skills. One of these doctors took a few of us aside and provided airway intubation instruction, which in our eyes, was exceptionally cool! It would be a number of years before services within Ontario would outfit the majority of frontline ambulance personnel with additional training, and the proper tools and procedures which would match the education of the paramedics we know today. With this background, I'm emphasizing that the EMS business as we know it today is relatively new, barely fifty years old compared to police and fire representation that has been around for over a century.

CHAPTER THREE

Can you write it if you haven't lived it?

Early in 1981, I applied to Conestoga College in Kitchener for the AEC program. Looking back while writing this piece, I can offer no solid explanation why I had applied to just one college which offered the program. One college? What was I thinking? But there were several positives about Conestoga College and while taking a liking to the general region of K-W, I decided to apply, and was accepted to this college. (That said, once I passed my exams and began searching for a permanent career location, I mailed out dozens of resumes.) Applying to one college was a decision I made on the premise that, if accepted, wonderful! Had I been declined, I had a plan to leave Canada and travel throughout New Zealand and Australia. (Again, just what was I thinking with that sort of plan?) Being kind of a free-spirited guy, who knows? But then, I could be writing on a totally different theme while on the beach in Tasmania, an island just south of Melbourne, Australia. Early life choices often set the tone for the direction of our lives.

Our classroom, located in the attached education wing of Kitchener-Waterloo Hospital, was typical size, with 24 students and shared a common hallway with the first-year nursing students. Their own classroom was directly across the hall from ours and from day one, it was somewhat of a constant distraction. The lead instructor and coordinator of the program (sadly, but with validity) offered periodic reminders to keep things on track; but what a fun time we had! The instructor was an intelligent man with a similarly sharp sense of humour which he radiated into his class daily. He was the guy who always 'told it as it was'!

Our program started in September 1981 and come January '82, myself and one other student were hired as part-time employees with the local ambulance service in Grey Point, Ontario. This was both exciting and scary, having just four months of schooling to our credit.

Yikes, the dreaded EMCA

Classes wrapped up the end of May, but the school work didn't stop there. All AEC students throughout colleges in Ontario began the torturous study marathon for the EMCA (Emergency Medical Care Assistant) exam. The written exam consisted of two, three-hour sessions on the same day, morning and afternoon. This part of the testing had the reputation of being an extremely challenging writing and the reputation extends to this day. Topics covered ranged from anatomy and physiology (A&P), sciences and chemistry, pharmacology, patient assessment and treatment, as well as legal policies. Naturally, the year previous students had given us the heads-up which topics were a big hit on their exam the year earlier but, as found by others writing subsequent exams, what we thought might be included on our exams received barely a mention.

Everyone has their own varied study habits. So, how does someone study for such a critical test, one which could potentially include material covered in the entire program? I definitely wasn't a model student in high school and I'm not sure how others prepared themselves, but I re-wrote my notes, not once or twice, but three times, all of them, start to finish, back to back. I concentrated on studying the way that I felt worked best for me.

Prior to 1992, graduates of the AEC program were not just responsible to complete the written EMCA exam, they were also required to complete two practical scenarios, which were equally as challenging as the written exam. Each scenario could range from a minor physical injury with a serious (secondary) medical issue, to a serious medical portion with a secondary problem of a serious physical issue. They mixed them up for us in so many different other ways, but you get the picture. It was a free-for-all!

I received my letter from the Ministry of Health (MOH) to attend for my own scenarios in London, at the Howard Johnston Hotel on Wellington Road. Once registered, anyone scheduled for this day was simply hanging out, waiting in fear in one area of the hotel, far away from where the action was taking place. When your time came, you were escorted to one of the hotel rooms in another wing of the hotel where you were provided a brief explanation of your call which was fictionally received from your dispatch centre.

We all knew this role as we had recently completed roughly 500 hours of preceptorship, nearing completion of our college program. During this period, we rode along with one assigned ambulance crew, on the real deal. While shadowing my crew, I observed them tending to those who were sick or injured, focusing on how they assessed our patients. I paid attention to the specific questions being asked while obtaining the patient's most recent medical history as well as anything significant from their past. Putting all this together enabled them to form their ideas on the chief complaint and any secondary problems. My preceptors had also graduated from Conestoga just the year before and, as I was doing now, they too had observed their preceptors at that time, and had since developed their own unique style of assessing a patient, finding their own groove. Every ambulance attendant had their own unique 'style' on how to determine what is going on with their patient. To this day, one of my preceptors and I exchange messages frequently.

You all know the size of a standard hotel room, which isn't huge by any means. Try to visualize this cramped scene: one patient, two ambulance attendants, and tons of equipment commonly found inside an ambulance, used to treat a patient. Then there were one or two others who may be present as bystanders, 3-4 others positioned (invisibly of course) about the room as the markers of the scenario, carrying papers and clipboards, who we were instructed to simply ignore (easier said than done!) Everyone in the room except for me, was already working as ambulance attendants within the province and were part of this EMCA exam team.

Some of those taking on the role of a patient also carried with them some unique talents. I knew of one young lady who was able to alter the size of one of her pupils, another could imitate absences of breath sounds in one lung, or part of a lung and others were able to contort their body limbs into some unusual, grotesque position. Each of these variations would challenge the candidate to the edge in its own manner.

Suddenly, I was up next. I was escorted from our waiting area to the testing site wing of the hotel. Standing outside the closed door of the room, I was told I had been dispatched to a hotel for an unknown problem in a local hotel room, no other information was available except a few words of encouragement, such as 'you've done tons of these calls already G, go get 'em!' No cue cards, no other info, nothing!

Each scenario allotted twenty minutes to get in, form your assessment, apply treatment to your patient, package them up (prepare them for transport), complete a (condensed) radio patch report to the emergency department, then also provide a more detailed report to the fictitious attending emergency physician. The focus of these components is to ensure that you, as the attendant, have applied all proper and appropriate treatments to your patient, which are all relevant to the chief complaint and determine other incidentals that you needed to figure out through your questioning. Markers throughout the room were observing whether you completed a thorough assessment of your patient from the beginning, including the dozens of fine details which were all relevant to the safety of your patient, yourself and your partner.

It was my responsibility to notice anything that appeared out of place. No one was there to prompt me or simply provide the information. This was my patient, I was in charge. The people in the role of bystanders in the room provided little information, unless you were to ask them. Prior to completion of our college course, we had been prepped on both phases of the exams and in this case, we were strongly encouraged to ask the bystanders as many relevant questions as possible. Naturally, any answers received may or may not have become a wealth of information. This was ours to figure out. We would also voice questions randomly, with anything we thought could be of importance, and the markers would reply accordingly. Upon entering the room, we might ask if there was any odour of natural gas present, the marker may answer, "no gases present", therefore you had eliminated one potential safety hazard and the markers made note that you considered/identified the hazard. Being specific was the key.

These questions and answers could provide critical information regarding the patient's condition, which could dictate subsequent treatments to follow. Earlier on, I mentioned the dozens of minute details which could include pretty much anything upon initially entering the room and scanning for hazards or threats: evidence of live wires, a gun, knife or other potential weapons laying nearby. Everything you saw, heard, or even considered was voiced out loud so the markers were able to make note of your observations. Makes sense why they had several of these invisible people placed about the room.

Should a candidate have missed any of the critical hazards which could have ultimately brought injury, harm or potential death to the crew or patient, this would represent an automatic failure. If one or both of the scenarios were classed as unsuccessful, then it was required that one or both would need to be re-done. Regarding the written portion: should the candidate have been unsuccessful with either the morning or afternoon sitting, they were required to re-write the entire six-hour exam. The EMCA testing occurred every six months and needed to be completed within one year of (successful) completion of the college course. A passing grade of 70% was required to be considered successful in the course and the EMCA exam.

By the way, we have only made it inside the door, just the first minute or so (of the scenario) has passed. Upon entering the room, I can see my patient and I'm already performing a visual assessment, even though I haven't even physically reached them. While scanning the room, if it hadn't been voiced or otherwise recognized as seen or heard, it could register as incomplete on the marker's check-list. The same applied with the entire assessment of the patient. Again, everything is voiced. Your initial and secondary assessments, everything is always hands-on. You are touching to feel anything which could be unusual or seem out of place, such as wet clothing or limbs in unusual positions, indicating external bleeding or fractures.

When taking a set of the patient's vital signs, I need to call out all my findings as I have determined, directed to the markers: what is their blood pressure, number of respirations (are they rapid, shallow, deep), breath sounds (do they have stridor, wheezes, crackles or are they clear) their quality as determined by listening to their lungs, how the skin appeared/felt (cold, hot, wet or moist, dry), colour (blue, red, pallor), any visible injuries or other abnormalities, pupillary sizes and their reactions. All which could indicate various health problems.

Depending on the condition and circumstances regarding the patient, the markers would come back with a different set of (number) values of vital signs and also different findings of my examination from what I had told them. This usually indicated a condition which might be considerably different from my own findings, and at times, required immediate interventions.

Thus far, I had examined from the patient's head, down to the chest on the anterior, posterior (front/back), and there remained the rest of their body. Front, back, sides including every area of their limbs and extremities. Your assigned partner, sad to say is pretty much useless. They cannot help you in any way to give the assistance which you would normally receive in the real world. You need to direct him/her to do absolutely everything, even how to go about wrapping a dressing onto a particular wound. In one of my scenarios, I asked my partner for a large pressure dressing which I needed to cover and secure an open leg fracture (gunshot wound), to which he replied, "Is that a four or six-inch dressing"? Really, man? You're getting on my last nerve!

I don't have the time nor the desire to get into the entire process of the practical portion, or else this writing would result similarly to a publication such as War and Peace. This explanation should provide a clear enough image of the intensity of the scenarios, and this is just the first few minutes or so.

I still have a copy of the two hundred or so voiced and hands-on must-do's which we were expected to address. This is the training we received and these routines were eventually ground into our brains as second nature. The more experience the attendant gained through their career, the more efficient they became in the completion of their assessments in the performance of their role in EMS.

At the end of the day following these two tests, I left the hotel with a firm belief that flipping burgers, becoming a theatre usher or jetting to New Zealand would be in my future, and honestly, I don't know any of my classmates who thought differently. These scenarios were that intense!

The practical portions were the second and final phase of testing, preceded of course by the written exam and we still needed to wait nearly two months for the receipt of our results, which would be sent out from W.A. Shooter of the Ministry of Health. We would receive either a thin or a fat envelope in the mail. Thin indicated a good news reply, fat, well… you can guess. I received thin, which provided a grade of mid 80's, covering both written and practical portions. This was good news as I don't even eat McD's burgers, although I do like the theatre and the beach.

A little advice. Don't rehearse for bad news or failure. If it's bad, deal with it, if it's a positive outcome, deal with that also. Anything else can be a waste of time.

I still held a part-time spot in Grey Point when I accepted a full-time position in Chase Township, Ontario, just two hours west of Grey Point, my hometown. Going from a college student three months earlier to being thrown into the full-time pool was a quick transition.

Working in the ambulance business at this time was a fast paced, high call volume industry, sometimes with few resources to provide back up for ambulance crews. Depending where you were in the county, assistance from a local fire department might not have been an available option. Firefighters during that time did attend with ambulance crews, just not as often as present day. When I began in the early 1980's, the ambulance service (which hired me) in Chase Township, stocked various other pieces of equipment which was used for light vehicle extrications. This included chains, 4x4 blocks for cribbing, and a block and tackle. Once we arrived on scene, if we realized we were well over our heads, then a fire department would have been requested to attend.

The block and tackle units we used were small, simple devices with steel hooks on each end and were somewhat larger than a common passenger car jack device used when changing a flat tire. We used the block and tackle at accident scenes in various applications, but primarily to pull the collapsed or mangled steering column of a vehicle, off a patient's chest, which had pinned/trapped them in the seat, thus restricting them from being safely removed. As mentioned, this device is small and when used in the above example, the unit's cable and pulley design can transfer enormous forces, such as moving steering columns and the like.

This usually meant, as ambulance crews, we were responsible for providing patient care as well as bearing the weight of extricating our patients from their mangled vehicles. Whenever this occurred, we hoped any other ambulances which were required at the scene were not a county drive time away. As you can imagine, this meant for a very busy ambulance call where you hoped for a great partner! (Our service in Chase was one of the only services I'm aware of which stocked their vehicles with these pieces of extrication equipment. We also carried kits which included pry bars, rescue axe, hacksaws, window punch, rope, which other services stocked their vehicles with. There were various other combinations which individual services put together to suit their own needs).

Weekend parties, with groups of high school or college kids out gravel running in their vehicles from one party to another, were frequently a test of our skills when they experienced a mishap. Gravel running = drinking and driving on the backroads, thus attempting to avoid the law. Not a great mix!

CHAPTER FOUR

Everyone in your life will have a 'last day' with you, but no one knows when that day will be

Here is one such example when an ambulance crew is pretty much on their own, with just the aid of one other crew. There were no supervisory/first response/jump vehicles to assist which may be part of today's ambulance fleets. In our area, it was not always common for volunteer fire departments to be contacted to respond and assist with vehicle accidents. It just didn't happen back in the day. Many of you might ask why wouldn't they be involved? This is just the way the agencies operated. Consider the period of time involved between the 1980's and our present day, the years in between and the time frame necessary to bring about such changes. Had our ambulance dispatch contacted one of these departments to respond, that service absolutely would have attended the scene. The guidelines reflecting any permanent changes in current policy can be a very time-consuming process to build, usually involving the participation of several agencies.

 A question and a statement follow, referring to why I remain so insistent on safety measures involving others, especially kids in various situations. Whoever thinks the lives of their loved ones, so precious, matter more than any price, raise your hand. Even more blatant, the lives of others as we recognize them at this moment can change, JUST-LIKE-THAT!

During one summer afternoon in the 1980s, my partner SC and I were returning from London on highway 401 after completing a patient transfer. We were roughly half way back to Chase Township, just laughing and chatting away while sipping a cold drink, saying we'd arrive back after our shift ended, which meant we could skirt around having to clean up the truck, once back.

No sooner as we were beginning another conversation topic, we witnessed a full-sized vehicle drifting towards the shoulder, approaching us on the opposite side of the median. This white vehicle produced a small cloud of dust when they hit the shoulder, the driver overcorrected which caused the vehicle to roll several times in the air, ejecting all four occupants within clear view of us both, all thrown out of their vehicle to the ground at highway speeds. On scene within seconds, we radioed dispatch of the situation and our location and asked for another unit to attend.

We asked for one unit because, knowing our location, we knew of a nearby ambulance station and had there been another truck already mobile in the area, our dispatch knowing this, would have sent them also. In present day, we would have requested three additional ambulances (one for each patient, total four), a local fire station, as well as air ambulance be dispatched. In a perfect world, had they not already been committed on other assignments, it would have been feasible to have them all attend.

We were fortunate the Rockway truck was available at their base. They were dispatched and would arrive within 10-15 minutes. All four patients were unconscious with critical, multi-system injuries which indicated (open) head wounds and injuries affecting their major organs (brain, heart, lungs), which meant all four had no doubt received serious internal injuries and hemorrhages. All four had a pulse and two of them were (somewhat) breathing on their own with varied respiratory patterns, indicating serious brain injuries.

While working such a chaotic trauma scene with just you and your partner, the two of you have a multitude of tasks to perform in a short period of time. This would include a survey of the immediate scene, followed by a triage, which is a process of sorting which patient(s) had sustained injuries more severe than the others. In this case, two of our patients had more significant breathing problems than the other two. The other two were breathing on their own at the moment, yet all four were critically injured.

Your initial triage, with four patients and two ambulance attendants should take less than one minute, all while openly communicating with each other followed with immediate treatment interventions for the injured patients. We applied cervical collars to all four (to maintain neck stability), inserted oral airways in all patients (to maintain an open airway), and applied dressings to their open wounds to control life-threatening bleeding. Our initial set of vital signs were also obtained on each patient to establish a baseline of their conditions. We initiated bagging procedures (IPPV's) to two patients and maintained airway suctioning to all patients (performing suctioning to maintain a clear airway) as well as administering oxygen to all, in a staggered sequence as there simply wasn't enough oxygen and suctioning equipment for all four.

Triaging: through triaging on this call, we simply didn't have sufficient man power and equipment to provide everyone with the utmost of continuous care. The triaging process provides us with the information to arrive at decisions, indicating (out of the four patients we had) which patients have the greatest chances of survival. In this situation, we examined a picture of four critical patients, of which two had worse respiratory concerns.

IPPV means providing intermittent positive pressure ventilations, meaning we are manually providing proper breathing rates and oxygen volumes compared with how they were breathing on their own due to their brain injuries. Bagging means forcing air into their lungs using a manual bag-valve mask device, which remains as standard equipment today.

Between the two of us, we were retrieving equipment from the truck: splinting kits, back boards to package two of the patients in preparation for transport. If we had the time, which obviously we hadn't, we might have begun preparing the other two injured patients for transport as well, but all ambulances in Ontario carry select standard equipment for just two patients. Ambulances stocked multiples of select items, but some of the limited standard equipment used for our injured patients was two backboards and one portable kit of oxygen (with additional oxygen cylinders) and suction equipment, which, back then operated using pressurized oxygen. Select ambulances were dual stretcher trucks, (outfitted with two stretchers) which were very useful for out of town trips and for calls like this, with more than one patient to be carried. All other units were single stretcher trucks. Every ambulance also carried one portable stretcher, a #9, which would have been used by the crew which was equipped with the one standard stretcher. Also, there was an obvious absence of IV kits, advanced airway equipment and cardiac monitors, which are all standard today.

With updated information conveyed to the second responding crew, it would have created a clearer image of what we had been dealing with, as well as updating the crew of any changes which had occurred prior to their arrival. Unfortunately, some ambulance services (including ours) had not yet been equipped with upgraded radio technology of the time, which would have included portable radios. This meant one of us needed to return to the truck to use the radio in order to provide any useful updates to our dispatch, which was then relayed to the responding crew. We were fortunate to have people who were travelling on the highway stop to offer assistance and we did utilize a few of them while preparing the injured to be transported. An OPP cruiser pulled up just as the second ambulance was arriving. The second crew, upon exiting their truck, brought with them various pieces of equipment which they knew they would need for the patients they were going to be responsible for. We provided the two attendants with an update on their patients' conditions, treatments rendered, and their vital signs, then finished preparing our own two patients for transport.

We departed the scene, heading back to London with our two patients, with each crew carrying one of the most seriously injured.

As mentioned, our ambulances carried a portable suction device which we used while next to the highway in the median. Inside the patient compartment of the ambulance was a wall-mounted suction unit with a reservoir to collect the liquid (and tissue) which was removed from their airways. For whatever reason, some suction reservoirs in the trucks could differ in size, and it's a good thing our unit was outfitted with a large one, approximately 30-40 ounces. Providing oxygen and performing suctioning to both patients inside the ambulance paints a picture of one crazy, hectic time. And it was! When suctioning in a situation such as ours, the suction reservoir would be maxed out in pretty short order and once full, no further suctioning can be performed until the volume in the reservoir was reduced, or in this case, emptied.

I advised SC of the situation, so he pulled over and stopped on the shoulder of Wellington Road in London. I then opened the side door of the truck and discarded the contents of the suction container onto the shoulder in order to be able to resume suctioning. Yep, right there on the roadside during rush hour. I kid you not!

The Dodge trucks back then were so much fun to drive. With more than ample power available, they handled well and were considerably smaller than today's units. I'm sure we topped out over 100 mph ☐ arriving at Victoria Hospital South Street campus in pretty decent travel time. However, we departed the accident scene at least five minutes before the other crew left, and they literally pulled in right behind us. It left no doubt that BP was driving. There were (and remain) strict policies in place within the MOH to monitor excessive speed (a vehicle's black box per se) however with instances such as this call, management would (frequently) let the infraction slide. However, that was then, this is now.

Two of the four patients died after arriving at the emergency department that afternoon. Summer weather conditions in this situation were clear and dry, but add rain or snow with subzero temperatures, the outcome could have been so much different. On a side note, events similar to this are not a rare occurrence. Not that they happen for a paramedic every shift, but in a block of their shifts, it may not be uncommon to experience such an incident. Some medics slip past these crappy calls, but for others, let's say some are labelled by other medics as a 'black cloud' who can receive more of their share of these kinds of calls. Some medics might welcome working alongside one of these black clouds while others would happily avoid such a partner. Remember, no one knows when that last day will be!

Fast forward 30 years, and much has been changed for the better. The industry sports a 'paramedic' designation which provides frontline workers several advancements including an array of medications used to treat multiple medical problems, as well as newer and better designs of equipment which are suitable for a host of incidents. It is evident that much has changed for the betterment of patient care in EMS, but one concern which has not changed until recently is how paramedics deal with the aftermath of difficult calls.

When I began my career, the owner/operators of some of the local ambulance services made it clear that if the attendants had a problem dealing with the after-effects of difficult or troubling calls, *there's the door!* That's the way it was, right or wrong. There was no room in the station for a debriefing. At the time, that term was rarely spoken but I do recall staff meetings where the owner would pass on a 'good work' message regarding a challenging call but nothing in the sense of 'let's talk about it'. So, as one might expect, we spent our time in the ditches, basements, apartment buildings and on the highways, completing the necessities of disturbing and challenging calls all while going about our business without an outward hint of distress. Wearing our game faces from the commencement of our shift to sometimes well past after it had ended, meant going home to loved ones and not a soul in your family was aware of the sights, sounds, or smells of the happenings during any given shift.

For those of us in the business of patient care, a game face didn't always hide emotion, as there were times when a troubling expression was noticed on the face of another responder while on the roadside, on a riverbank, in a residence or in the emergency department. Even hospital staff would sometimes display a troubled look; everyone is entitled. Many of the seasoned medics had been around long enough and didn't show much sense of distress but not all who worked in that time period were stone-faced. We knew who we could open up to and those to avoid. That said, once in a while, it was a gruff one who was actually more approachable than the others and a quick talk now and again seemed to smooth things out and answer some tough questions.

Looking back at the years I have invested in my own career and at the paramedics who were, at the time, ten or twenty-some years older than me, there is no way that some of these ladies and gents weren't also suffering in silence. During down time back at the station, the conversation would inevitably include ambulance calls which some of the more seasoned guys had been part of over the years, some references dating back into the seventies or even the sixties. Being newer, I had seen my own, smaller collection of nasties, but some of their own stories would leave me shaking my head. There's not a chance that they were somehow unaffected. Not a flipping chance!

I know of some coworkers who left their positions without warning or explanation, but it left us with plenty of speculation. At the time, with my own very few years invested in EMS, I would have had no idea that several of these events were related to a psychological cause. I can also surmise that the province's distilleries never missed out on a banner year, as myself and several coworkers happily contributed to their cause.

I am not criticizing the owner/operators, I'm simply addressing the fact of how it was back then, because we now know so much more about the relationship between mental health and EMS.

CHAPTER FIVE

Critical Incident Stress Debriefings / Peer Support

Critical Incident Stress Debriefings (CISD) are used by emergency service personnel after a traumatic incident that has been determined to have the potential to interfere with the worker's ability to function in their role within emergency services. The debriefing is usually conducted within three days of the event and is designed to enable workers to return to their routines more quickly, lessening the chances of experiencing PTSD due to the incident.

In 1991, myself and a few others attended a course in basic and advanced CISD models where we received training by Maryland, USA physician, Dr. Jeffrey Mitchell, who developed the Critical Incident Debriefing Program. We were part of our local CISD team which unfortunately disbanded after just a short period due to a cut in funding. The dedication of the three individuals who donated many of their own hours running the program also realized their primary careers were suffering, when they needed to spend their weekends playing catch-up, resulting in exhaustion. Ultimately, the team folded and sadly, none of the other local agencies stepped up to help keep it afloat.

In the early 2000's, after an incident which had been determined serious enough to warrant a debriefing, select agencies imposed mandatory attendance for those who were directly involved. For a two-year period, I was part of a police communications centre and while with this service, a large-scale incident occurred which resulted in approximately forty personnel from several agencies taking part in the debriefing. It was quite the event.

Again, with the same service, another incident occurred which affected many personnel within the entire service directly, including a handful within the communications section. Whether it was the administration of the time, or other factors that were responsible, but speaking for us as civilian members of the service, we were well taken care of in many respects to the incident.

There are agencies locally and internationally which continue to use debriefings, together with peer support services, as their own way to de-escalate after serious incidents. Agencies which continue to utilize debriefings use an enhanced design of the older, original models and have added trauma trained psychologists as facilitators.

No Bad Crews, Only Bad Leadership

Years ago, I was one of several paramedic crews who worked a tragic water rescue/fatality. Afterwards, many of us were collectively hopeful that a debriefing could be organized. This could have included multiple, allied agencies which participated that evening: First Call Emergency Medical Services, Sterling Falls Police Services, Sterling Falls Fire Service, and OPP (police), to mention a few.

After speaking with others, I emailed a member of upper management within our service where I requested an incident debriefing for all involved. In his reply, he denied us the debriefing, stating that in place of CISD's involving frontline first responders, statistics indicate using peer support networks (which outweigh the use of debriefings) and are generally the preferred therapy. A peer support network? What is that?

What really disillusioned several paramedics who were on the river that night, was that no one within management on any level had tried to contact any paramedics who responded to the incident, to inquire of details of the incident or our safety in general. Incidentally, there was no management representation of any level present on that call (which was unusual). I will say that management was contacted by a few medics that night shift who received negative comments related to their requests. Back in this time, our service did not retain a peer support team, nor had there been any related correspondence circulated through the service regarding any such idea being considered, developed and launched. Yet, a member of management from the service had looked into and researched the matter.

It is our understanding that the local hospital conducted their own debriefing as did OPP, city police, as well as two fire services. It's also my understanding management representatives from our ambulance service attended the hospital meeting.

Thank you to those who made sure my partner and I were all right following the call that night. I don't think this crew was present as they were holding down the city, running the calls in town. My daughter, who was living with me at the time, called two hours after my shift was to have ended to see if everything was okay. I provided her with some basics of the accident, advising that I'd still be another two hours. There were serious consequences due to the actions and inactions of our management at all levels, and had nothing to do with the mental toughness of any paramedic that responded to that incident. It was shameful, to say the least. When there is an enormous task sitting on the doorstep, there are no EMS personnel who are able to simply turn and walk away.

This call on the river would bother me for many years and I know for certain (through conversations) that it has troubled several others belonging to various agencies. This is the nature of this beast; it is common for EMS workers to not open up and discuss these types of apprehensions. (Hence, the reason for requesting a debriefing.) I know there are exceptions, but sadly 'opening up' is not as commonplace or accepted as first responders would prefer. However, talking about sensitive issues in safe places eliminates the shame.

Just days after the river call, our management advised that all ambulance personnel who attended the accident were required to provide a statement to Sterling Falls Police Service. The proper legal forms were in place, permitting us to discuss details of the call with a third party for purposes of the investigation. When it was my turn, I must have provided a boatload of information because my interview was ninety minutes long whereas the others who gave statements did so in a mere fifteen minutes, so said the interviewing officer.

For some reason, I felt I had a personal stake in this, which I informed the Constable in part of my statement. Maybe I had a sense of what might be coming up because on the way to the call, I removed everything from my pockets including my cell phone and wallet. It wouldn't have been the first time I had entered a body of water while with EMS. As we arrived on scene and descended the long, steep grade from the roadway towards the water, I observed a police officer standing mid-thigh in the cold water. We recognized each other and he spoke first when he said, "I'm not a strong swimmer." I replied, "I am." I removed my coat and duty belt, removed my boots, ready to enter the water. He handed me his flashlight which I stuck it into the waistband of my pants.

The vehicle headlights were visible through the murky water and I estimated the car to be approximately 30 feet from shore and maybe 20-25' below the surface. This was mid-December; I wasn't aware of the water temperature but I knew the La Grande River carried a reputation of having a strong current and I was trying to determine how far upriver I would need to enter the water for me to have the fast current push me downstream toward the headlights where I would then dive down to the vehicle.

In fact, I was a strong swimmer, certified in (NAUI) SCUBA, had swam competitively for years, had made snorkel surface dives to beyond 20-30' but only in calm, warm waters, or in a controlled environment. Although I was in decent shape, I was many years older and definitely no longer maintained the swim physique as before. This was definitely not a controlled setting and I was relying on the water current to provide me with, at minimum, the momentum I needed. After quickly processing this information, I was suddenly overcome with a thud of rationalization: the water temperature wasn't near freezing but was still damn cold, the air temp was close to 0C and I could visualize the fast-moving current. I was wearing my duty pants, long underwear, shirt and T-shirt. Through various water rescue courses through my early years, swimming while fully clothed can be a challenge much greater than one might imagine.

I remember all I could do was let out one loud curse! I redressed myself and carried on with the task at hand which was assisting my coworkers with two patients who had managed to swim to shore. Considering all factors, I had suddenly realized my intentions were futile, unreasonable and potentially deadly. Through the months and years, I would carry an overwhelming sense of guilt which would include images of the headlights which continued to beam through to the water surface, knowing there were still others inside the submerged vehicle.

There was no subsequent in-service follow-up in reference to the river call. No staff meeting, no formal union intervention, no direction on how to establish a much-needed support team. Nothing, not even a wellness check. After the river call, there was at least one other paramedic I know, besides myself, who approached senior management with a request to develop a support program to assist paramedics in need after attending disturbing events. Nothing came of that request either. To top it off, it would still be another 7 or 8 years before preparations for our own Peer Support Team would begin, as unreal as that seems.

Green-Yellow-Orange-Red

Without the proper education or in-service training on how paramedics can avoid becoming psychologically affected following tragic calls, we were all pretty much functioning in a near-blind state. We hadn't yet been provided the training or knowledge what the signs or symptoms of psychological trauma might appear as, which could indicate who was in a (green) safe zone or who was within a critical area (red zone) on a mental health scale in our world of paramedics.

We all have safe options available to us. There remains an onus on the worker to seek out guidance and direction from any member of their agency or anyone who maintains a capacity to lend competent assistance.

April 2016, government bill 163: WSIB in Ontario was mandated to recognize and accommodate emergency service workers who come forward with a concern of PTSD, without requiring the worker to provide proof of a specific event which caused their condition. The client was still required to make their way through the process as always.

I have known of emergency workers, prior to the 2016 mandated decision, who were in long, bitter and almost hopeless battles (their words) with WSIB while attempting to have their claim resolved. I do not know specifics on the former, however, there are others who had simply given up on having their case approved. They had decided it was actually less stressful to continue to live their life mentally affected and distressed, while being supported emotionally and financially by family. Having opted out and signed off with further involvement with WSIB, they would not receive any form of benefits to cover treatment, nothing! There have also been incidents when workers in similar circumstances had decided to take their own lives. This is a matter of serious importance.

Any worker can become deeply affected and overwhelmed in a relatively short period of time. What happens if one of our own has become affected over the past few days/weeks and has now isolated themselves and none of their coworkers (or family connections) have been able to recognize the signs of their crisis? Remember, everyone has those options available to them 24/7: a crisis line, 911, your local emergency department, contact/call a friend or family.

Early 2018, our spring in-house training was, in part, focusing on how to identify the warning signs of PTSD in a coworker, those possibly experiencing a mental health crisis. During one of the exercises, there was a role-playing activity and while one of the instructors walked about the rows of tables, he stopped suddenly right across from my table and while looking directly at me he asked, "Do you have PTSD? Are you in a crisis situation"? While looking him straight in the eye I answered, "Nope, not me!" (You just can't make this up if you tried).

Hats off to our in-service trainers and management for having the foresight to include this crucial information as a training topic. Generally, those with a background in psychological trauma would maintain an edge in distinguishing key signs, but this training opened another door with hopes for paramedics to be able to recognize something just wasn't right in someone who may be in trouble.

While on the road at work the following day, my partner said I could have turned that moment right upside down had I provided a different answer to the trainer's question, relating to my very own condition. We continued to discuss other possibilities, especially when the information in one of the handouts had identified me in the red zone, at a critical level and clearly in a crisis. (A fact which I was already quite aware of.)

We both knew this was definitely no matter to be laughed at. It was also interesting to note, with all the paramedics in the room taking part in this mandatory training, no one was able to pick up that at least one of their own was in a serious mental health situation. Just one more example how I (and others) have been able to mask any obvious indicators of my condition. After all, I was within my work environment and had brought along my game face, and once the course was completed and I was on my way home, everything would change again!

Many of the paramedics present for the training were from my own shift whom I would cross paths with, sometimes several times per shift. One clear fact exists - PTSD remains a problem with all first responders and I know first-hand that it can sometimes take a skilled worker to identify someone suffering or being affected.

Side note: After I had taken my leave, a friend and fellow paramedic confided in me that prior to me going off, we had spoken several times either on the road or in hospital and at that time, he too was at a critical level. He had been in active crisis and neither of us were able to spot the signs in the other. We each knew that the other was PTSD affected, but it wasn't clear that we were both at a crisis level at the time. This is very scary stuff when considering the sheer number of paramedics and other first responders within the Province of Ontario who may very well be in similar situation.

CHAPTER SIX

Our brains are wired for connection, but trauma rewires them for protection. That's why healthy relationships are difficult for wounded people – Ryan North

In early 2016, I was attending couples counselling to address a relationship concern and during our second session, the counsellor suggested there was more going on which indicated PTSD rather than a specific relationship conflict. Within days, I received a referral to Mrs. Lorraine Wilson, and soon thereafter, I began treatment.

The thought of PTSD had not even entered my mind as being the culprit of some of the issues I was experiencing. There was one person within my own circle of friends who offered their own opinion, challenging the suggestion of PTSD. They were implying there was no way I could have a psychological injury, after all, I was still working. What? Where did that notion come from?

That, of course, has become part of the misunderstandings and the stigma which exist to this day! Going down the road through treatments, Lorraine Wilson and I were able to recognize several indicators that my PTSD condition dated as far back as pre-2000. Twenty years ago, without the knowledge and ability to recognize the signs of PTSD, they were cast off as being so many other possibilities, such as relationship conflicts, lack of situational coping mechanisms, work-related issues or other mental health issues including anxieties and depression.

Even today, it is evident that many of the issues I was experiencing back then were classic symptoms of PTSD. Through treatment, I also learned that in relationships where both people are affected by their own specific circumstances, this can present a very poor mix, creating an unhealthy, toxic environment. I am so thankful this counsellor was able to pick up on my condition.

Withdrawing or pushing others away may well be someone's manner of finding comfort and peace within themselves while they struggle with their mental health. It can also be an indicator that they are struggling with PTSD.

This distancing from one's own family can happen in many ways. There is a valuable lesson learned from the following scenario: a paramedic has a full-time position with their primary service but it isn't uncommon for them to put in additional shifts at a secondary paramedic service. Many of these secondary employers require their part-time employees to work a minimum number of shifts per pay period, which may include weekends and statutory holidays. These shifts are worked during days off from the paramedic's primary service where they are already logging an 84 hour (two week) pay period. There was only a handful of years when I had just one employer; all other years I had a minimum of one part-time ambulance gig on top of my full-time job, which took me away from family and home life for extended periods. This would include family holidays and occasions that, once missed, you could never get back again. This has me shaking my head, wondering why I did that, especially when my kids were so much younger. We can always consider our regrets, but it changes nothing.

When I began my career in the 1980's, few attendants secured these secondary employment opportunities and if they did, it usually was not related to ambulance work. Later, when some of us did find that second EMS job, many of us were just happy to earn the extra cash, especially when the needs and demands of family life became all that more pressing. Through this reflecting, I realized something of disturbing interest.

When looking back at my own work history, the years when I was working two part-time jobs, logging hundreds of additional hours on top of the 2,080 hours with my full-time position, these were the years when several of my symptoms first presented. So, if withdrawing and distancing myself from family was an established way to cope with my PTSD symptoms, then me working two or more jobs is no coincidence. In retrospect, I wish I had made more sensible decisions, ones that had solid meaning.

It should also be no surprise that just 4% of full-time paramedics reach their retirement age while still on the job. That figure was around when I first started in the business and it has not changed to the present day.

I first noticed this distancing in my marriage with the mother of our two children, when it seemed I had entered into an unfamiliar depressed state, and I struggled to find any happiness in my life. At the time, I found my comfort in alcohol which seemed to cast a welcomed numbness over me, thus (partially) eliminating the toxic thoughts related to my work life.

Over the year, it was clear our personal lives had taken a back seat and before we knew it, we looked at each other wondering who we were and how had we arrived at such a sad stage in our lives. We had two beautiful, gifted and active children, busy with full schedules which involved mainly sports activities. I addressed the subject with my wife and she was direct and to the point:
"You have some major issues G. You're pretty screwed up!"

I knew I was pretty messed up.

Still, without any idea of what could be happening, I made an appointment with my family doctor. There, I explained my concerns regarding my marriage and I left his office with a prescription for an antidepressant. My doctor at that time also worked shifts in the emergency department at our local hospital, so he knew I was employed in emergency services. Unfortunately, however, there was no discussion about the correlation between my role in the ambulance service and the condition I reported to him. Widespread psychological trauma within EMS was still barely a consideration in our industry.

After leaving my doctor's office, I filled the script, popped a Zoloft and off I skipped. I was truly excited, believing my life would rebound back to normal in no time, and within a few months, I would once again be able to enjoy all the happiness which once surrounded me.

We had an amazing family life on Canyon Circle. There was love, laughter, bickering, family stressors and pressures, midweek volleyball and hockey out of town, all while addressing high school academic necessities. Our home was usually the hub for family gatherings, specifically when serving turkey or hiding Easter eggs. I so loved my family but I knew something wasn't right with me and I believed my wife when she said I had a big problem; a problem which I knew wasn't figureoutable! (Yes, it is a word.)

(I knew you'd look that word up). A few months went by with me taking Zoloft and my wife and I continuing our marriage counselling sessions. I had suggested we go this route with the hope of finding a solution or even a reason why my life seemed so chaotic and my wife agreed to attend. Unfortunately, within a year we separated and I have not been very forgiving of myself for making that fateful step of separating.

I wasn't unhappy with my life, but I was a man affected with a psychological illness. Yet, within the world of emergency services, I remained too young to interpret the important signs and symptoms I was experiencing. My former wife has since remarried and I will point out we have a positive relationship; we're all family, her husband states. When we gather for family functions, it puts me at ease knowing our son and daughter don't have to be on guard and some of their friends still cannot believe it's like 'business as usual' at family functions. I definitely feel blessed.

CHAPTER SEVEN

Little did I realize, some of the events and horrific scenes I had been subjected to over the years prior to the breakdown of my marriage, had set me into a downward spiral. Once a shift had ended and I returned home, it was important for me to be able to detach from my work and any nastiness which had been part of the shift.

With no logical or established process for these situations post-shift, I chose the alcohol route, as had others I worked alongside. For me, it delivered its familiar numbing effect, and I went with it. Earlier in my career, I was able to drink alcohol socially and more sensibly with my family, coworkers and friends. Taking a look back, the frequency of drinking (and the amounts) increased over the years. Add to this the volumes of negative and troubling incidents, I unknowingly continued to pack all the bad into a vault in my mind, to be retrieved another day. I wasn't aware of the serious damage I was inflicting on my family and can only imagine the stress I was creating, and like a virus, it would spread and contaminate our home.

Complex PTSD, sometimes referred as C-PTSD, occurs when someone has experienced repeated or prolonged periods of psychological trauma which may also involve incidences of abuse experienced in childhood. I have always remained cautiously reluctant to provide deeper descriptions of certain circumstances directly to my family. This decision is based solely on protecting and shielding them from some of the results faced by someone who is affected. (However, as we recall, shame takes a backseat when disturbing stories are told in safe places).

Some of you have heard me mention the name Mrs. Lorraine Wilson. She is my counsellor whom I see regularly for therapy. Lorraine Wilson is a remarkable woman, humble and kind. She is extensively trained and considered an expert in EMDR therapy. She currently promotes this therapy in conferences throughout North

America and also provides EMDR consultation to EMDR therapists internationally, via Skype.

Eye Movement Desensitization and Reprocessing (EMDR) is a psychological approach which has been extensively proven as one of the treatments of psychological trauma. This design of therapy isn't for everyone, yet I have experienced positive results. It helps me to function in my daily life with the circumstances involving PTSD. Eventually, with this and other treatments, one day I could very well be free from the shackles of PTSD. The science behind EMDR really works! I am grateful for Lorraine Wilson's help and you will read about her throughout this book.

There will always be non-believers in our industry, unfortunately. There are paramedics and other first responders who maintain the notion that what has happened to me will not happen to them. There's a good chance that I, too, was one of those who couldn't see that the tables would turn. Many years ago, as far as I was concerned, I was fine mentally. Without hesitation, I disregarded the quirky psychological thoughts and hadn't given a second thought to the possibility that some of those disturbing events would be silently accumulating within my own vault. Never say never, people.

Years ago, I recall reading some excellent articles about those who became affected with psychological trauma but I had no idea how serious, troubling and debilitating it could be or could become. The symptoms I experienced were insidious and silent. As mentioned earlier, they can be missed or mistaken as other emotional or situational concerns, as was the case for me.

I had no idea of the impact this would have on my life and the life of my family, or how rapid some of the symptoms would progress and eventually snowball once I hit that critical point. You have no doubt heard the phrase, "your cup runneth over". Speaking as a paramedic, this combination of words can be used when referring to someone who has reached or is near their mental breaking point, generally as a result of becoming overwhelmed in a specific set of circumstances. Coming to grips with the realization the contents of my own cup were nearing its brim and that I was affected with a workplace injury was difficult for me to comprehend, and it also frightened me.

CHAPTER EIGHT

If you're going to tell us how to do our job, then shouldn't you at least know how to do our job and the consequences of it?

I feel a need to touch on a subject which rears its ugly head from time to time in the industry of first responders. When signing up for an EMS career, we obviously knew or we should have known, that we would encounter the obviously unpleasant aspects of death. But we were quickly introduced to sheer volumes of death, tragedy and mayhem which all ambulance crews experience. When referencing, 'we should have known', it wasn't intended on being humorous. It isn't common, but over the years we've had students or even new hires who have suddenly dropped out of the course or resigned their position after attending a few of the 'holy crap' calls.

One example of such a call is treating a child who is barely more than a toddler, who is clinging to life after accessing a parent's drug paraphernalia and has ingested residue from their pipe, straw or a spoon. Whether you're a seasoned medic or fresh out of school, that's a tough call to attend. Often, it's EMS, the police and hospital personnel who are subjected to such a call and the public rarely hears about these dark events. Our world is not the comfy, cozy picture postcard many believe it is, or should be. Once again, any and all who are associated with the treatment and investigation of this child have one more dark event to file into their own vault. Who knows, while being a black cloud in the business, maybe it remains one of the reasons I'm in the spot I find myself in now? More on that later.

However, there are those among us, who act as armchair directors who sit on the sidelines far away from the action. Some would prefer to comment or provide illogical references about topics which they know little to nothing about. These people are more commonplace than even they are aware. Possibly it's their shallow, perverse interest/excitement regarding death, but it's disgustingly bothersome!

"What did you think you'd encounter in an EMS career, you moron. You signed up for this." We're aware of how troublesome, challenging and heart-wrenching some events can be and the toll it takes on everyone involved, from paramedics all the way into the emergency department. The ER doctors, nurses, lab technicians, diagnostic imaging, department clerks, psychiatric, ICU, pharmacy, right through to discharge planning are all too familiar with the regular happenings. So, when I refer to tough calls, we know it's our job and we perform it well. Getting back to these armchair directors though, some might be quick to point something out to us through argumentative tactics or some are just (ignorantly) curious. They wouldn't ever want to become any part of a hideous scene, yet they could be the very ones who just gotta get closer for a look-see!

CHAPTER NINE

He's also having a very rough shift.

The following is an appalling true story, one which is more common than many believe. **Caution: May be triggering.**

Nearing the latter part of the 1980's during a winter storm, an accident on highway 401 resulted in a double fatality. The vehicles involved had been travelling in opposite directions and one of the vehicles had crossed the median, striking the other head on. We were the only ambulance crew on scene along with two OPP cruisers. One of the police units was positioned down the road in the eastbound lanes alerting oncoming traffic of the hazard ahead. The wreckage and scattered debris were restricted to the median and passing lane which slowed traffic that passed next to the destroyed vehicles. As mentioned, the traffic approaching the scene had slowed considerably, yet there were the rubber-neckers. Rubber-neckers are the inconsiderate drivers who congest the accident scene by slowing their vehicle even more, some even stopping to check out the destruction. This creates yet another traffic hazard, potentially jeopardizing the safety of all emergency workers present.

This accident happened decades before the 'move over' campaign was introduced, which eventually had the HTA (highway traffic act) amended to make it the law for drivers to move over if able, leaving one lane's distance when emergency services (including our towing services) are working on a roadside incident. It is extremely unnerving to have traffic passing at highway speeds within four to five feet (sometimes even less) while workers are performing their duties on the roadside. Prior to the campaign, we can all recall some ridiculously close calls and one doesn't realize how close the potential for death really is! Had this accident happened today, this section of the highway might have been completely shut down to all unnecessary traffic.

Our two patients were not going to be transported by ambulance this night. Close your eyes and create an image of the scene - on a dark stretch of the highway with two extensively damaged passenger vehicles, car parts strewn about, traffic continuing at a much-reduced speed. Most of the drivers are respectful while passing through, aware of the additional hazards. However, there are others who believe they are permitted to get a closeup of the violent crash which has taken two lives. Two such vehicles passed by at a crawl, nearly stopping. It was quite disgusting! One of the police officers (out of old district #1 detachment) had just about enough of the blatant disrespect. He began yelling at the drivers, "You want to see this? You want a closer look?" I know the officer and the rest of what happened, but I'll end this story right here.

Two adults had instantly lost their lives that evening. These patients were someone's son, daughter, sibling, spouse, possibly even a mother or father. They had both been loved by others and others had been loved by them.

As a first responder, this is sometimes difficult to convey to others, but this is true about our work. It is our job to view and handle the dead or dying but we do it with dignity and we perform this more often than any of us would prefer to acknowledge. I'm sure many others can vouch, and I know I have had enough ignorant people suggest, "You're used to it. You see it all the time." Which is possibly why these others perform the slow drive-bys, just to catch a glimpse of something awful to satisfy their curiosity. How else can one describe it?

If you think everyone is a fan of EMS, you best rethink that thought. Remember the argumentative arm chair directors I mentioned? Several times, too often to remember, upon arriving at a location where an ambulance had been summoned to help someone, we experienced unjust scolding or have been harshly reprimanded for our tardy response. If a verbal lashing wasn't sufficient, we have been pushed, punched, spat on and threatened, all in the name of not arriving a few minutes sooner. And I'm certain every police officer can attest to the same, unwarranted treatment.

I definitely remember times, pushing that envelope just a bit too far sometimes when sarcastically asking the angry ones, "You know we're not the police, right?" This response was sometimes an ice breaker but it wasn't always a game changer. And believe it, once in a while, something physical would follow. Several incidents come to mind as well as the partners I was with at the time. There were calls when we found ourselves in situations where we simply needed to defend ourselves, which we most certainly did! As previously mentioned, at this period of time, not all services within the province were outfitted with portable radios to call for assistance, and our service was one which did not; which offers explanation of the dust-ups. Paramedics and other first responders being assaulted is a serious and widespread problem, not just locally and within our country, but on an international scale.

All paramedic crews are subjected to their own stretches of dreadful calls. During the years 2015/2016, my partner Holly and I worked through an especially challenging period when we attended several tragic and distressing calls. These calls would affect us both in profound ways and would send me a signal that I could soon be looking toward the end of a career which I had embraced and been so passionate about.

It is a common realization for paramedics, and in fact all first responders, that each of us are just that 'one call away' from ending our career. Our roles involve physical and mental work, either of which could contribute to a career-ending injury. I know of paramedics who had their career come to an end as result of serious back, shoulder or other joint/muscular injuries but fewer whose career ended from a psychological injury. I know the latter are out there, we just don't hear of them as often. When referring to the rarely spoken psychological injuries, I suspect this is due to lack of awareness, too subtle indicators of what to look for, and/or more commonly, those simply refusing to admit to having such an injury, due to the attached stigma. This could include frontline paramedics and even management personnel within the services.

There have been coworkers who, after much consideration decided to painfully ride out their career instead of considering their options, such as seeking treatment. I was never concerned about the stigma of 'coming out' with my situation. I never worried about being looked down on, as being weak. I wanted to know what was happening to me, I wanted my life back!

 A few friends/coworkers have reached out, crediting my efforts in bringing forth more awareness of my own situation, which ultimately affects thousands of others. One such friend was direct when saying, "Good for you, G, for speaking out, as many of us are too embarrassed!" Now doesn't that speak volumes on its own? Never say, 'that won't happen to me', as life has a funny way of proving us wrong.

When we welcomed the year 2018, I sensed my life was beginning to spiral dangerously out of control, like a corkscrew into the dark earth. This new year wasn't shiny and bright as in the past, with party hats, horns and celebration. I viewed it as just another day, another start to another year. While already in treatment, I was beginning to realize that treatment alone wasn't going to be enough to keep me from being further affected, or worse. I did eventually make a conscious decision that if I wanted to remain mentally safe, I needed to walk away from my career, and to do so soon.

CHAPTER TEN

The 'wow' list.

Trigger point:

Mid 2017, during a treatment session with Lorraine Wilson, she explained it was necessary for her to know about specific types of incidents which have caused mental struggles. She asked me to comprise a list of 'categories' of calls I have attended. As it would be impossible to address and treat each and every troublesome event, she asked me to come up with a checklist which she was able to place into her own arrangement for purposes of treatment. Once back home, at my grandfather's desk, I began documenting these incidents and it was strikingly clear that the volume and nature of calls that I have attended over the years was far greater than I might have imagined. Some of my work friends have asked various questions regarding my condition and asked for an example of treatments. I recall discussing this category list with one very seasoned crew. After explaining what was required, it took mere seconds for one of my friends' eyes to be as wide as saucers as he realized the volume of events which he had attended (and possibly the subsequent impact those events had on his own life and the lives of his family). The two of them exchanged glances while distantly reflecting on a few such events and it was obvious that I had unintentionally triggered them.

As expected in our work, there are situations where there is absolutely nothing we can do for our patients. These patients are men, women, boys, girls, mothers, fathers, someone's brother, sister, aunt or uncle. Literally, everyone loves someone else and are loved by another. With this in mind, I want to explain that while in attendance of many of these situations, some of us, including me, prefer to function in an auto-pilot mode. I identify this as a personal safety factor. If we were to view these situations in a strictly human sense, there is no way we would be able to do the work we do, call after call, day after day.

While sitting with pen in hand, I was blown away with the vast assortment of incidents we had attended. I'm sure you, too, are able to use your own imagination regarding what sort of scenes most paramedics and first responders attend. Gunshot injuries, hangings, drownings, choking patients, motor vehicle and industrial accidents, incidents involving multiple patients, patients dying due to natural causes, structure fires. Then consider the child abuse events, spousal attacks, sexual assaults, burning vehicles with their injured occupants trapped inside and unable to free themselves, calls representing a true threat to the lives of the paramedics at violent and uncontrolled scenes. Many of these deaths and the circumstances around them were so damn preventable! Some of these calls number in the dozens, and many in the hundreds, literally.

As EMS workers, we have attended multiple events which have involved the use of a firearm and there have been incidents which involved firearms directed at us specifically. One such example involved walking up a narrow set of stairs of an apartment within a house and upon reaching the upper floor, I found myself looking down the barrel of a .38 handgun. Another incident involved a shotgun, an over-under shotgun to be specific. One was in a residential area, the other in a rural setting. It kind of makes perfect sense why entering a rural property for some calls would give me the jitters throughout my career in some of these locations.

There have been other situations while tending to injured persons in rather volatile settings, we were able to catch the sound of the hammer of a gun being cocked as we assisted an injured patient in a crowded scene; we were told we weren't moving fast enough for those onlookers. Several examples of the above occurred in the 1980's when it was common to respond to many (sketchy) areas of concern, minus police assistance. Important side note: the men and women in blue have been there and saved our butts (as paramedics) many times throughout my career. For that, we are indebted.

Over the past years, I recall several local paramedics relating their own stories of attending calls, only to make a hasty retreat while the bullets were flying over their heads as they took cover behind a vehicle. Or, as in recently while in a crowded bar setting, quickly vacating a scene with our patient to avoid a potential personal assault. These types of situations can occur even after taking all necessary precautions. All you have to do is ask any police officer or EMS worker in larger communities. One of our guys had experience working in the USA, where such occurrences were much more common. There are so many other incidents where, as EMS, we had staged far enough away from a dangerous situation awaiting word from police that they had the situation contained and it was safe for us to enter.

Trigger point:

Paramedics obviously deal with many different types of tragedy but when asked, most will admit kid calls can be some the hardest to work through in grievous situations. These calls involving pediatric patients happen at a lower incidence compared with adults, however, they are an entity all their own. I know paramedics with fifteen plus years of service who have not experienced a pediatric death on the job. Other paramedics are not as fortunate. Speaking for myself, by the time I had eight years on the job I had directly dealt with nearly a dozen incidents which resulted in the loss of a child, and five of these were in a span of just eighteen months. Tragic accidents, SIDS, suicide - these calls are always highly charged. Children are supposed to possess a future and are a never-ending hope for their parents, being so cherished. One point to clarify, is that children I'm referring to in these tragedies can range from newborn to age seventeen. Very sad!

Come to the end of that eighteen-month stretch, I knew I was most definitely affected by these deaths but dismissed the anxious and numb feelings as, 'all part of our work' (as we had so been earlier reminded). Up to the end of my career, I would also encounter several others. Some may ask, how is it possible we are unable to remember each and every tragic death, specifically involving children? This is just another example of the mind blocking out extremely disturbing thoughts and images for us, as explained by Lorraine Wilson. This, too, is science-based fact. Another example to consider: I cannot recall each and every shotgun death or injury I have attended.

We've talked about some of the various challenges faced by paramedics and I know for sure, some of my weak points will be another's strengths, and vice versa. While working in EMS in an ambulance, you are partnered with another. The longer you work together, the more you learn about each other and become familiar with the other's work habits, including the strengths and weaknesses. After time, we can work through many serious and challenging calls, sometimes with minimal communication necessary. I know this goes beyond EMS, stretching into several other allied agencies.

CHAPTER ELEVEN

Death Notifications (past and present day)

One particularly challenging responsibility of our work involves death notifications. This is where paramedics will inform family or friends (when present) of the death of the patient, where the crew has tended to the patient. Remember I mentioned being in autopilot mode? The best way to describe this, is processing and working the scene, maintaining our composure while wearing our game face.

Back when I began in the business, there were few protocols to dictate when we would not transport a patient, thus leaving them where found. In that period, there were three defining circumstances in which the patient remained at the scene: someone who was decapitated, transected or decomposed. These were classed as obviously dead; seasoned medics may continue to refer them as code 5, in like circumstances. Almost everyone else was given a ride to an emergency department, whether dead or alive.

This would occasionally present situations when specifics of a call were pretty much divided by a very thin line. A thin line, not so much with our definitions within the MOH guidelines, of whether to leave a patient or transport them, but when the police were involved. The police, specifically an attending sergeant, didn't always recognize our ambulance guidelines, so, when a patient did not present with one of the three 'dead' classifications, our mandate required us to transport. To the police, if the patient was intact, even warm but dead, police wanted them left as part of their investigation. We get that and we generally also knew when someone was dead, but rules are rules. However, when we agreed to leave the body, we had an officer in charge sign our form acknowledging these facts. Only then would we leave the patient where they were. On that note, we encountered some officers who were pretty much unimpressed!

Here is some rationale to consider involving just one patient: EMS has arrived where someone had requested an ambulance to attend. We gather a history of the patient's chief complaint, conduct an assessment and depending on our findings, we initiate the appropriate treatment and transport them to hospital.

Or, we gather a history of the immediate circumstances, conduct an assessment, obtain a history of the setting and the nature of the patient's medical or traumatic presentation. Dependent on our findings, we would initiate treatment while still assessing the gravity of their condition/injuries, and initiate a telephone consultation with an emergency physician who is working in an emergency department within our area. With collaborated efforts of the paramedic and the doctor, we discuss the setting, circumstances/nature of the call and our treatments rendered. With this information a decision is made during the telephone consult and we continue our treatments and transport our patient to the hospital, or, we cease treatment; we do not transport the patient. At this point, we give the death notification to those present, explaining what is usually obvious to us, but not always to others.

Resuscitation measures are fast moving and aggressive, and from the view of a non-medical person, they can also appear intrusive and violent. This may or may not be the way family who are observing this process care to remember their loved one. That said, for a number of years now, hospital emergency staff have allowed (select) family members to be present during the resuscitation efforts. Respectfully, there are family who wish not to participate in this activity, and there are others who choose to witness that everything possible is being done to save the life of their loved one. This can lead to a very positive and lasting memory.

While comparing similar events within the controlled environment of an emergency department, when paramedics arrive on scene at a residence for example, we are sometimes faced with a very different scenario. It's not always just the paramedics who attend the scene;

fire services and police may also be present to assist in various roles, which often creates a very crowded, hectic area and these scenes can understandably be highly emotional for family or bystanders.

When a decision has been made to cease resuscitation, this is the period when a notification will occur. We make every effort to preserve the dignity of the deceased and respect for immediate family/friends present and explain the decision to cease treatment.

For a paramedic, being responsible for delivering news to a family of their loved one's passing can be a great challenge. There is a powerful impact on us to assure the selection of our words of explanation do not inadvertently create additional suffering to the survivors. Not all notifications we deliver will be the same. There may be similarities in the deaths, but the survivors we speak with are all individuals with no similarities between them, which makes each notification unique.

This is an integral part of our role as paramedics, yet we were not provided instruction or training on delivering such tragic and important news. It may not be common practice but it isn't unheard of for police officers attending at a death, to request paramedics remain on scene to assist with the notification. Example: a young adult has died in a motor vehicle collision and the victim's parents who are on their way to the scene will soon learn their son or daughter has passed away. As with any surviving family, these parents are deserving of kind, empathetic words explaining the death of their child. There are no words to reduce grief in any of these situations.

I have worked with many medics who are extremely kind and sincere, who routinely take those few extra minutes with their patient and others present. There are also those in this field who present with less empathy than others. This doesn't always paint them as a bad person in their field. There is one more thought to consider, which is pretty straight forward.

Everyone in their own profession, occupation or whatever business in which they earn their living, provide their own 100% effort. Everyone's effort will vary because we are all individuals, we're all different. It isn't always a clear balancing act.

Several months before working my last set of shifts in May 2018, I noticed a pattern had developed while being at work and when I was off duty. While away from work, anxious moments combined with an eerie, familiar numb feeling would be present. In wide comparison, while working out of my own office, which of course is my ambulance, it still amazes me how the mind is able to continue to operate efficiently when first responders, who harbour deep levels of anxiety, hypervigilance, depression and whatever seems to come about, are able to function within their role, dealing with situations requiring great focus and concentration. Yet, once my shift had ended and I am on my way home, my ability to remain as the mentally strong guy vanishes and switches like night and day. It made the swap to the other G; someone with genuine human traits, someone who is much more vulnerable.

Over a few years, my partner and I attended numerous grim calls which resulted in the death of several patients who had met their demise either by accident or by their own hand. Having been in my career this long and having attended hundreds of these incidents, I was mindful enough to realize I was clearly becoming much more affected by these incidents than before.

Paramedics, like other first responders, attend thousands of incidents over time and quite robotically, without a second thought, file these traumatizing sights, sounds, smells and anguish deep into the vault within our minds, hoping to never see or hear from them again.

For the first time I could recall in my career, I was coming to grips with the fact that I was now unable to force these unpleasantries down into the secure vault and out of sight and mind. I was no longer able to ignore the images of the grotesque scenes, which I usually forced down into the vault, along with hundreds of other events. I began to notice I was being weighed down with overbearing emotion. Until now, I had attempted to labour on, call after call, day after day, the way I had for decades. I became quite accustomed to these transformations and at the end of one such day shift while driving home, it hit me! I could clearly notice the shift, which was usually quite abrupt, and this occurrence had me laughing out loud while acknowledging that Jekyll and Hyde are alive and present. I can even remember where I was on my way home that day.

For those who aren't familiar with those names, they are one, the same individual, Dr. Jekyll and Mr. Hyde. Dr. (Henry) Jekyll has an alternate personality who is Mr. (Edward) Hyde (this is me at work, but I'm not evil). These are fictional characters from a novel written back in 1886. Dr. Jekyll battles the good and bad within himself, leading him to struggle with his alter ego, Mr. Hyde. I think you can see why I compared myself to these fictitious characters.

This is also a deep-rooted quality with first responders who are affected. Thus, being at work IS my happy place and likely reflects any number of paramedics who continue to work and function in this environment, yet outside of the lights, sirens and chaos, they too may also face very similar struggles at the end of their own shift.

CHAPTER TWELVE

Your therapist doesn't fix you; they are there to help you fix yourself.

Knowing how necessary it was to leave my work was troubling enough, but once we closed the door on the year 2017, the now undisputed stack of 'why I needed to leave' arguments was overshadowing the 'maybe I could stay on' reasons. I knew that I needed to apply greater focus to the steps I had been avoiding up until now. As we entered the first few months of 2018, I was even more assured that my career, one which I had been so passionate about, had been a serious, ongoing contributor to the decline of my mental health.

Recently, I realized that I had lost my ability to ignore the warnings of disturbing images, signifying being unable to deal with sensitive, highly charged events. Unknowingly, I was entering a period of surrender, waving my white flag! I had entered into yet another dark period, a pattern which never seemed to end. Should I accept this as a positive sign or was it simply a continuation of so many other negatives?

Select blocks of my days off, days when not in uniform, were filled with anxieties, suicidal ideations, alcohol and depression. I dreaded the thought of leaving my friends at work. Not just within EMS but also those associated with other agencies we laboured alongside, day and night. I enjoyed friendships/acquaintances with OPP, city police and fire fighting personnel. I knew if I had ever cared for my health to become manageable, there remained only a single option and this was the timing I had been awaiting.

Lorraine Wilson and I had discussed leaving work on a number of visits yet I just didn't know how or when I was going to go about doing it. When we discussed my leaving, she offered encouragement in various ways; supporting me mentally during this life altering decision. Saying adios to a crappy occupation would have been an easy call but I wasn't in that position.

Several times, while in the course of my treatment, she'll give me that look, which means through all the darkness, turmoil, pain and sadness, I already know the answer, a solution to a current issue. I've found myself backed up against that imaginary wall within the comfort of her office many times only to once again realize it is only me who can discover new meaning and understanding; that we all have an inherent ability to heal ourselves. Everything is within our power. Finding a solution for this challenge was no different. This was a major decision to be made. A major decision that could bring a profound difference to my life.

Three days before my 60th birthday, I found myself working my final shift in the career I had started nearly thirty-six years earlier. My career had come full circle; having begun as an ambulance attendant with Chase Township District Ambulance, a blended career as an Ambulance Communications Centre (CACC) supervisor and paramedic to where I was today as a front-line paramedic. There was also a period as a shift supervisor on the road in Chase Township where, the truth be known, I did not enjoy this period of my career. I decided to accept this position when it was offered, primarily because the alternative would have left me with lower seniority and less of a wage. Most of the people I associated with were an amazing bunch; a few others, not so much!

Back in Sterling Falls, my partner Holly and I have been avid supporters of each other throughout the years, always looking out for each other during mentally draining times. And, although torn, she was also a supporter of my own decision to leave EMS. In conversations over several months prior to leaving, she admitted she had noticed the slightest of changes in my personality; some I had been aware of, other times I had had no clue. We valued the time working alongside each other and as much as she'd rather I stayed on, we both knew the longer I continued to work on the road, the greater my mental health would be affected.

Our working relationship was solid enough that discussing sensitive issues was never a struggle, it was just part of another conversation. We had been partnered five years and had developed a strong bond, especially over the previous twenty-four months while weathering those several difficult and troubling calls. Within EMS, not every partner we work alongside affords us the opportunity to develop a strong, trusting, confident partnership but when fortunate to find the right fit, one should never take it for granted. I know of several strong paramedic partnerships and through the years, I have been able to work alongside one or the other, which makes it easy to see how some crews seem to work so well together.

As most paramedics in a long career, we have worked with many different partners and spent many thousands of hours in side splitting situations in the cab of the ambulance, which most always involves sick, stupid, dark humour which only select others can appreciate. I recall several incidences, where the joking continued all the way up to the scene of a call, only to verbally remind each other (Sinkie, Mike, Satan, CL, JM, LS, BS, TM, DP and so many others I simply cannot mention them all) that it's game face time, time to get down to business. Nothing like pulling into a local emergency department at 2am for an out-of-town transfer while head-bopping to Queen's Bohemian Rhapsody all while being spotted by the family of our soon to be patient. These were fun times for sure!

Anyone working as a first responder knows all too well that just because your shift is scheduled to end at 1900 hours, this carries no guarantee that we'll be able to sign out and head for home once the clock strikes seven bells. We also know that anyone working these shifts who has concrete plans after work, might as well set yourself up for early disappointment. The odds are, you and your partner will get tasked with yet another call while on the road and at the mercy of dispatch or, you will be paged out just in time to spot your relief crew driving up the street toward the station as you, inside the ambulance, are pulling out on your assigned call. Never fails! Go figure.

Let's not forget another part of end of shift. While cleaning up, we were always careful to not begin cleaning up and washing the truck too soon near the end of shift, which would in all certainty jinx our opportunity to avoid that last-minute call. This was definitely reciprocal, but I remember Holly asking me, "Where do you think you're going?", which usually meant take a seat (don't jinx us), the truck can wait. Generally speaking, one of us had plans after work and wanted to avoid a last-minute call and leave on time. As said, this admonition worked both ways.

I had to laugh at her humour. On more than one occasion, she threatened to banish my son Chris from stopping in at the station for a visit near our shift end, while he was on his own way home. No sooner had he left, yup, we'd be paged out and a few times we even watched him pull over as we whizzed past.

This evening's crew change was different. There was none of the usual chatter and bantering between us about events through the day or whatever came to mind. There was an unusual, somber mood in the air which was not picked up by our (incoming) relief crew. Generally, when being relieved by another crew, we might talk about events of the day which could include equipment, stock, technical or vehicle concerns as well as the everyday dull and uninteresting chit chat and again, sick, stupid humour and laughs, most always at the expense of someone else. In that regard, today was just another day of crew relief. I finger swiped out on time, with no shift overrun, which wouldn't have made any difference to me on this day. When I left that day, May 22nd, Holly was the only one who was aware that I wouldn't be returning, and in the minds of our relief crew, all four of us would be returning for our next scheduled block of shifts beginning Friday.

But I had other plans. Two weeks earlier, I booked an appointment with my family doctor, and on that day, the day after my final shift, he would sign me off as being unfit for duty. Today, a tough day, one which left its mark, being the end of my career; definitely not the way I wanted to go out! No bitter feelings, no sadness, just emptiness! Buckets of it!

The other crew and Holly and I had been together for several years now and I had thought about bringing them up to speed with my plans for the next day and why I was leaving. But, there were just too many variables to consider. It definitely wasn't the proper setting to open up with, "It's been great working with you guys but I'll be (sort of) quitting my job tomorrow!" For these two who were just beginning their shift, it would have been horrible timing to drop such information. I know I wouldn't be up to receiving such news. Dropping a 'Debbie-Downer' statement like that would have been simply too inappropriate. A few weeks later, I did stop by the station and offer an explanation and the facts pertaining to my departure.

CHAPTER THIRTEEN

A life altering appointment on a bright, sunny morning.

The following morning, May 23rd, it was warm, sunny and bright when I arrived at my doctor's office, twenty minutes ahead of my appointment. After nervously checking in with the office receptionist, I took a seat in the waiting room with other patients. My mind was racing, feeling like I was about to do something illegal. Was I making the right decision? Had I considered every possible option or appropriate resolution to all of this?

Should I go back and tell reception I made a mistake and can't do this right now? I knew that wouldn't work because when arranging the appointment, she needed to know the nature of the visit and naturally, I had been honest and told her, 'I didn't think I was able function properly while in my work environment any longer'. On that note, I would have been in a heap of a mess had I decided to leave the office.

I felt panicked. I slipped into the bathroom and caught a reflection in the mirror. I saw someone who clearly wasn't me. This fella looked scared and agitated, pale and aged. While shaking my head, I told myself out loud I needed to calm down and pull myself together, while splashing my face with cold water. I returned to my seat in the waiting room, still considering making a dash out the door. Instead, I fumbled through some useless pamphlets, something related to bladder dysfunction and COPD issues. My name was called and I follow the nurse into an office where I had my vitals taken. Again, I'm asked, "What brings you into the office today G"? Again, I feel no shame or humiliation and tell it like it is.

"I've been experiencing difficulty coping while at work." They all knew my occupation, which didn't make it any easier. I find it easy to talk with most people and I've had many conversations with this doctor's office personnel, but I find myself struggling with these uncomplicated words. Oh, and what a surprise, my blood pressure was higher than usual!

I am led into one of the larger offices followed by my doctor, Dr. Bernstein (name has been changed). Dr. Bernstein is a tall, big man, with a hoarse, gravelly voice and can offer an intimidating sense about him. During past visits, I've taken note and sensed he seems uninterested in my condition. I took a seat and as usual, he makes things light in the office but it's discouraging he doesn't follow up on my progress with the medications he prescribed just a few months earlier. Like, "How has your anxiety/depression been since we started the new meds? Any new changes? How's your sleep been?" Isn't this referred as a follow-up inquiry?

Doctors, while in their offices, are not supporters of idle chit-chat with their patients. They have a structured time period to follow, to reduce the backlog of those waiting to be seen. Conversely, I have had docs in the emergency department stop me just to chat or a question about my well-being. Just a difference in how everyone operates, but it also shows that the ER doctors are demonstrating a different kind of interest. *A personal interest*. Imagine that! So, there in my doctor's office, I explained the issues I've been experiencing while off duty; the same concerns which might also be creeping in and affecting the performance of my work. I tell him I believe it is time for me to step away from my job; to sign off permanently. While I am anxiously pouring my heart out reflecting my current situation, I am looking right smack at the side of his head. He stops typing on the laptop, turns to me and says that once he completes and signs the necessary forms there is no turning back; there is no magical way to undo this. He is respecting me by offering this explanation, yet I feel I'm being scolded with his tone.

I acknowledge his statement and at the same time, wonder if he has actually been able to see through me and interpret the serious personal crisis I'm experiencing at the moment. Why can't he just stop recording the facts for two short minutes and have a personal face-to-face conversation with me? It crosses my mind that he may be incapable of holding such a conversation.

Occasionally on other visits, he didn't have a problem initiating several minutes of idle chatter. But, like this morning when there's big money on the table, he's either missed it or chosen to ignore it. Maybe I'm just another person on his list of the morning's appointments. Again, this situation had me wondering if I'm doing what is best for me and it was crystal clear I'm on my own at this point. I won't be receiving any guidance from this guy today.

Dr. Bernstein continues with the paperwork and asks a question, a question he is mandated to include. Without making eye contact, he asks if I have been having thoughts of suicide, or considerations of hurting myself, to which I blatantly lie and answer no.

For a split second, I wonder if I should really annoy him and ask, *what if I had answered yes to suicidal thoughts!?* I guess it's quite possible I would have been persuaded/forced to go to the local ED, and with the local police at that! These officers, many of whom I know as friends or acquaintances, would have uncomfortably transported me into the emergency department, the same department I have attended hundreds of times. Once there, of course, I would find it necessary to retell my story to the all too familiar nurses and doctors, many who are friends.

Nope, not a hope in hell that I was going to go down that road and I knew in my heart that there was a more 'user friendly' way to begin this adventure. As the doctor leaves the office, I hear his usual, "Have a good one, G." He handed me a stack of forms to pass on to his receptionist, who would need to make copies for me before I left the office.

 As far as I was concerned, and at my request, Dr. Bernstein had just signed part of my life away, and he leaves the exam room with, "Have a good one, G."

His comment left me speechless.

CHAPTER FOURTEEN

What's next on the day's list.

I left the office and headed for one of the popular food establishments which we regularly visited many times on brighter days while on duty. I picked up what I needed, got into the car, started the engine, put the car in gear and then just sat there frozen, staring, unable or willing to feel any emotion. *What the hell happened? I just cancelled my career and I have no emotion to show for this action? This is too bizarre!*

I took the car out of gear, then shut the engine off. I didn't even crave the items I had just picked up, likely through habit. Total silence surrounded me, oblivious to the traffic and pedestrians around me. The moment was a solid reminder how I was feeling; totally numb to everything. I couldn't have cared less about what would happen next, recalling how meaningless I felt moments earlier in the doctor's office. I felt absent of all emotion. I had never been permanently signed off work. I'd taken time off for a physical ailment sure, but certainly never a mental issue, which in itself was a sobering, frightening and unpleasant moment in my life. What was my next step? I guess I needed to let someone know I wouldn't be showing up for work in just two days for my weekend block. Obviously, that just might be an important next step. I needed to try to work through this beautiful sunny morning.

I had always maintained a decent rapport with the management of First Call Emergency Medical Services, but knowing who today's on-duty supervisor was, I wasn't comfortable explaining my circumstance to him. So, I opted for plan B. I decided to call Travis who was probably in his EMS office where he conducted his own day-to-day business.

Being mid-morning, it was anyone's guess where he could be, so I took my chances and told Siri to give him a call. I was hoping Travis not only answered but was actually nearby, as I wasn't feeling the warmth regarding having to discuss my present situation with either of the other two top dogs, who had offices one floor above his. He picked up right away and off to his office I went. It was a relief when he picked up, as I also wasn't up to leaving voicemail messages or chasing him down through texts with such a sensitive issue.

Travis and I have known each other many years and have attended calls together all while maintaining a good working relationship with him in his role in management and me as a frontline paramedic. He's easy to talk to most days, but depending on the subject and situation, that man can be all business. He welcomed me into his office and I took a seat in one of the chairs across from him, leaving the door open as usual. On earlier visits, we joked around, sarcastically kidded each other, but not today. Today was very different. While tilted back in his chair he greeted me with, "Hey, what's up man"? I stood up, closed the door and took my seat on the edge of the chair, just looking at him, seemingly not knowing where to begin. Travis leaned forward and started it off when he asked, "What's going on, G"?

I'm sure we talked for half an hour while I revealed my current situation. I had been diagnosed with PTSD for almost one year and had been in treatment for a few more. Travis listened respectfully, took notes and asked several questions. It left me confident that I had chosen well when I decided to speak with him on that beautiful sunny morning. During our talk, there were periods when I noticed him just shaking his head in disbelief that this paramedic and coworker was affected with a psychological injury and no one had noticed the signs.

Union leaders within our organization had suggested that when having conversations with management, keep the details few and to the point and whenever possible, arrange for union representation. Over the course of my career, I have experienced work-related physical injuries which necessitated employee/management meetings. However, I recall just one or two incidents when I asked a union steward to accompany me. I was always up front and honest and chose my words carefully and never experienced an issue that resulted in a negative outcome.

This conversation with Travis carried enormous importance, yet, given the weight of my circumstance, it never occurred to me to consider having a union rep accompany me. The instances when I had arranged a union steward in the past was based on whom I had the meeting with, not the incident specifically.

What's the saying? When it rains, it pours?

Evelyn Thoms (name has been changed) is my case manager with WSIB who is part of the Mental Stress Injuries Program. She handles my case files and receives progress reports from Lorraine Wilson as well as from my psychologist, Dr. Roberts (name has been changed). Bear with me, this starts to get interesting.

I first met Dr. Roberts in the summer of 2017, when I was initially assessed by him over a course of three visits, which formally acknowledged my diagnosis of PTSD. Evelyn Thoms, with WSIB, advises she has not received a progress report from him since January 2018.

Since then, Evelyn Thoms advises that she has been attempting to contact Dr. Roberts regarding the progress reports she has not received, however, weeks have passed, with emails and voicemails remaining unanswered. Lorraine Wilson had forwarded her own completed reports to Evelyn Thoms as requested; however, Dr. Roberts is the registered psychologist and WSIB is not permitted to accept the interpretations of Lorraine Wilson's reports without also having corroborated reports from Dr. Roberts, which they have not been receiving. Lorraine Wilson files her own reports under the supervision of Dr. Roberts.

Evelyn Thoms also mentions in our conversation that she has received several reports from Lorraine Wilson, yet, we all know the content of the reports could not be formally interpreted without the blessing of Dr Roberts. Yes, it's screwed up; a bloody mess of sorts which had my head spinning with irritation.

When I was first placed under the care of the mental stress injuries program, I was assigned a case manager whose name was Brian (name has been changed). The days when Brian would call, I was always left with the feeling that my needs had been taken care of. I felt he was a compassionate man, a good listener, with a genuine sense of empathy. It would have been an added bonus to have had him assigned to me as an ongoing representative.

Unfortunately, within a few months of my coming on board, Brian was replaced by Evelyn Thoms who, when asked, explained it is common practice with WSIB to rotate their case workers among their clients. Most days, I would regard myself to be an open-minded person, providing the benefit of the doubt whenever necessary. Shortly after Evelyn Thoms first introduced herself, I had envisioned all kinds of red flags, but I made the effort to allow her to display her true colours, as just possibly, she had some genuine kindness tucked away, somewhere.

Every three to four days, I would receive a call from Evelyn Thoms with an update, that there was no update. She had not received any new correspondence from Dr. Roberts. With no other reports to consider, my claim remains unchanged (unapproved). That was disheartening news.

May 22nd, was the day I left my station for the final time. Not long after I had left work was my birthday. While alone in my home that morning, the air around me didn't convey any hint of a very happy birthday feeling. However later in the day, that would all change and become so much brighter.

Without the relationships I have with my children and my grandchildren, this day might have been just one more day of turmoil. However, with us all celebrating together at my daughter's place, it made this day full of happiness, joy and colour. Even for just a few hours, the break allowed me to escape the darkness which had surrounded me earlier in the day.

My daughter Randi, son Chris and son-in-law Marcel, along with Tyler, Devon and Ava have been my life savers. Earlier in this book, I talked about how difficult it is to spot someone who is affected. Well, the last thing I ever wanted to pass on to loved ones is any hint of how serious and unmanageable my condition can be. Sufferers of PTSD can be masters at hiding our feelings, and for some time, the true me remained unexposed to those who remain so close.

Realistically, I knew the recent reports which had been faxed from my doctor's office would not likely have been received/reviewed by my caseworker and it had me wonder, where would the funds, my pay, which I had been receiving every two weeks from my employer, come from now? I obviously needed a source of income to meet my needs. Why hadn't I been able to consider this sooner?

I met with Travis again to explain what was happening, or rather what wasn't happening with having my claim approved. It would have been easier to have simply called and discussed the details over a phone call, but while growing up, I was taught a valuable lesson by my mom. She had obtained her business degree from the University of Toronto by the early 1950's so she was up on the business do's and don'ts and any business etiquette. She maintained that arranging an in-person meeting regarding any important topic is not only more personal, it demonstrates that effort was put forth which can further define the significance. In this instance, I was hoping for someone to help me, so I would definitely make the effort to see him.

While I was present, Travis made a few calls and advised me that First Call EMS would cover my wages until my claim was approved, but it was made clear they would not do this for any extended period. To make it even more thought provoking, should my claim be denied, I would be responsible to repay all monies received to bridge the gap. This was fair, and made complete sense.

However, while I struggled mentally each and every day, the thought of potentially having to repay such a sum of money was of serious concern to me.

Shift workers are notorious for poor sleep habits, what with being up all hours of the night, running all over while much of the population sleeps. This goes totally against the grain of normalcy, in my mind anyway. A sound sleep has always been hit or miss with me throughout my career, even with the assistance of sleep aids. I began using Zopiclone several years earlier when having being up all-night running calls then coming home and being unable to shut my mind down and drift off for some quality sleep. I also hadn't realized until years after, but this medication was designed for short term use, and, due to the highly addictive nature of the drug, it was no longer legal in the United States.

Much of this crazy insomnia seemed to surface when a few of my symptoms first appeared, but once again, I was unable to recognize them as I can today. I continued to use this medication for several years until they were eventually replaced with antidepressants which also helped bring on sleep. Stopping the Zopiclone cold turkey (as my doctor suggested), instead of gradually reducing the dose of the medication was a brutal experience which, fortunately, didn't last as long as it could have.

As with anyone with a mental health concern, finding a proper balance of meds can be a significant, lengthy challenge. Since my diagnosis, I had been working with my GP, Dr. Bernstein, trying to find the appropriate medications and dosages for my condition.

Through trial and error, even when I was able to manage some decent sleep, it would now be disrupted with nightmares which included random and disturbing work-related events. To my relief, Dr. Bernstein referred me to a local psychiatrist who took over the management of these medications.

This was truly a feel-good moment for me, and here's why. Dr. Bernstein had prescribed a few medications to manage my condition, and, over the first 'few weeks' of taking one of the meds, after discussing it with him, he made a significant dosage adjustment of the medication. This new dosage, within just a few days, dramatically worsened my condition. I spoke with my pharmacist who verified my concerns, who then contacted Dr. Bernstein with another recommendation. I'm certain this was one of the reasons he arranged for the psychiatrist to take over.

In my opinion, it might be safe to suggest that he might not have been within his comfort zone working with mental health patients who required psychiatric medications for their well-being. In his defense, he wouldn't be the first family doctor to feel this way regarding patients like myself and our psychiatric needs. Thankfully, that's all behind me now.

For those who have worked with their health provider and have experienced the trial and error of determining the best suited medication and dosage for your needs, you know it can be an arduous period with enhanced periods of highs and lows. For those who at some point could realize the need to travel this road, I want to suggest to do your best and be patient with the process, it is common for this to take time! As recent as February 2021, I again worked through a change in one of my primary medications and this period also presented with its own frustrations.

CHAPTER FIFTEEN

Over twelve months prior to leaving my job, I had been experiencing frequent mental triggers which involved an increasing number of circumstances. There was simply no way of avoiding them other than remaining inside my home, only leaving when absolutely necessary. A kind of life that could somewhat resemble house arrest or a lockdown (prior to Covid restrictions). I had to take things slow and steady, one day at a time. Not to mislead you, but I continued being out and about, as there was no way I was going to voluntarily close myself inside and subject myself to this house arrest business.

I went through a total knee replacement in late 2019 and for a one-month period post-surgery, I found myself leaving my home solely for the purposes of physiotherapy or other necessary appointments. After the thirty-day period, and once I had received the go-ahead to drive again, I noticed some of my triggers had lessened to a point of nearly vanished! I hadn't recognized the absence of them until I was out, leaving the house again, and entering our wide and wonderful world. Of course, they would present themselves anew, depending on the situation.

Just a few examples of the triggers which come to mind: marked crosswalks with their flashing lights, with adults and children waiting for impatient drivers to come to a stop before being allowed to cross the roadway. Dense fog conditions in the morning while everyone is on their way to work and school, school buses with their stop signals and light systems activated while students are boarding or exiting the buses, absurdly loud vehicles, fast and reckless driving by thoughtless, inconsiderate drivers. These few examples represent deep associations of violent tragedies which ambulance personnel everywhere have experienced. Yet another few dozen files to bury deep down, to deal with another time!

Shortly after city planners activated a desperately needed set of traffic signals for pedestrians in the north part of my city, an acquaintance on my street was complaining one day. His beef? "Just one more delay to getting where I was going." After replying, "It's not even a two-minute delay on such a busy street," all I received was a blank stare. If he only knew the circumstances of the misfortunes which had occurred at these various crossings.

On the subject of dense fog, I have a story I want to pass along. In the late 1970's, one of my best friends was critically injured in a car accident one morning during a dense, heavy fog. Her family lived about 20 minutes east of Grey Point and she was driving herself to school in town at the time. She was initially transported by ambulance to Grey Point General then transferred to Toronto General where they began to treat her for a TBI (traumatic brain injury).

She would require several months of intensive therapy: relearning a vast volume of tasks which we all take for granted, daily. We were both in our final year of school and I made the trip to Toronto a few times per week, doing what I could along with her mom in MG's hospital room. Prior to her accident, we would spend time just hanging out in Grey Point or, some weekends on her parents' sailboat docked in a slip at Port Credit Marina. We also took in trips into Toronto/Mississauga and of course, people watching on the dock at the marina, while enjoying cold bevies. Fun times they were, and thankfully, MG made her full recovery.

Trigger point:

Recently, a close friend who resides in a rural area of Sterling Falls, extended an invitation to my two oldest grandkids to come out and ride a smaller version of an ATV which his own son used to ride when younger. The boys would love such an opportunity and George wouldn't have offered if he had any safety concerns. George is also a paramedic and knows all the risks. The ridings would take place on his farm, far from the busy highway which runs past the front of his property. Once again, I know this would be a safe and exciting time and with the ok of their mom and dad, I'd take them out and they'd have a blast.

However, the moment he mentioned the invitation, my mind was taken back almost thirty years to an incident involving kids and harmless fun, one summer afternoon. Not an ATV, but a motorized fun toy all the same, also on a rural property. The kids had a problem starting the ride so, as most kids had been taught, they bump start the machine: with someone pushing, and, while the machine was in gear, pop the clutch and once enough speed was attained, off you'd go.

In this case, it was possibly pushed further up the driveway than intended and once the motor started, the novice operator, who didn't have enough experience with the present circumstances, was unable to stop. He crossed onto the highway at the end of the driveway, directly into the path of a semi-truck. Things happened so quickly, and we'll leave the incident right here. With no disrespect to anyone associated with this incident, but here is just one example how first responders cannot, as much as they'd like, avoid mental triggers, sometimes having them occur years, even decades, later.

CHAPTER SIXTEEN

What just happened here?

Recall how Evelyn Thoms of WSIB hadn't had much success in contacting Dr. Roberts for his current progress reports? She called to advise me of yet another delay. WSIB had determined the note which Dr. Bernstein had written explaining why I was to be off was, in fact, too vague. And, unbeknownst to me, other documents WSIB received from his office indicated I was to be off for a period of just four weeks. Maybe this was the standard he was required to follow, but there was no explanation provided at the time. Unfortunately, the problems didn't end there.

While in Dr. Bernstein's office that beautiful sunny morning in May, one of the documents he handed me was a note explaining why I was to be off work. After reading it, I questioned him regarding his choice of words; I told him I didn't think it included sufficient details for others to arrive at a clear decision. He assured me the note would be fine and I left the office, feeling certain his note would be challenged.

Evelyn Thoms continued to say that should my psychologist, Dr. Roberts, be unable to submit the necessary reports, WSIB would arrange a comprehensive assessment in Toronto within the month. The idea of having someone else hear my story again wasn't sitting well with me, so, that afternoon, I drafted an email addressed to Dr. Roberts and bbc'd to Lorraine Wilson, which read, in part:

"Against your advice, it will be necessary for me to attend and be assessed in Toronto at CAMH in early August. With these results, I hope to have my claim reassessed as it has not been approved for the purpose of receiving financial compensation. My WSIB case worker, Evelyn Thoms advises that your January 2018 report has been the only report submitted this year and as result, there remains no other criteria upon which to base any changes with my condition. Additionally, up until May 22nd, the day I left work, there is no documented evidence from you that my condition has in fact deteriorated, except for notes received from Lorraine Wilson, which, as you know, cannot be considered as they have not been endorsed by yourself. I have now determined that someone with a BSc degree will decide my fate (by having me attending CAMH in Toronto). I have been advised there is established policy which you did not follow and Evelyn Thoms also stated, without hesitation, "Dr. Roberts failed you, G."

Just one year earlier, in the summer of 2017, when I first met Dr. Roberts, I concluded he could be a strong, reliable resource whose reports might just provide an uncomplicated transition resulting in an approved WSIB claim. Instead, I was left feeling alone, hung out to dry with no explanation from anyone.

I completed the email draft that afternoon but I did not send it. The following day, I attended his office, hoping to speak with him, yet was once again disappointed when his staff simply advised he wasn't in.

I felt as though I had been thrown into a dark river of rough waters with no one to call out to, with no visible means of an exit. I felt like a drowning man and I had no idea how close I actually was to being in a predicament as such. When I returned home, I closed the front door, silently sitting alone. I was in a deep sense of despair yet I was able to recognize how desperate I was in the moment in an attempt to see any solution to this ordeal. Many random thoughts darted about inside my head and among them all, I wasn't able to find one logical thought. I sent the email that afternoon and shortly after, I accepted a call from Lorraine Wilson. We discussed the option for an independent assessment and she was upfront when she stated she had no idea why Dr. Roberts was unable to be contacted, as she, too, had made attempts.

Following the call from Lorraine Wilson, I placed a call to WSIB, advising Evelyn Thoms we had decided to go forward with the appointment in Toronto and Evelyn Thoms also told me I would be placed on a cancellation list. Additionally, I was offered an even earlier spot in Sudbury or Thunder Bay. I decided to wait the additional 10-14 days (or whatever the time span was) for Toronto. I consider Toronto pretty much local anyway, with travel time being less than three hours.

The next morning, I was stunned to see an email from Dr. Roberts. He stated this situation was very upsetting to him and if necessary, he will send another report to WSIB and address this again, and to leave it with him. Really, another report?

Here's a laugh: years and years ago we had a boss who forever used the same phrase, "Leave it with me"! It's a joke to many of us because we rarely heard back from him either!

Days later, yet another email came in from Dr. Roberts stating he had reiterated in correspondence to Evelyn Thoms of his recommendation to not have me attend CAMH. By now, I knew Dr. Roberts's ghostly involvement in this matter was finished and I was heading to CAMH. I was also bewildered and didn't know who or what to believe.

Dr. Roberts stated he had left messages and had been playing phone tag with Evelyn Thoms. Evelyn, on the other hand, stated they have no record of any incoming phone calls or voicemails received from him. Also, she had tried no less than seven times between January and July to reach Dr. Roberts, and the internal psychologist had made three attempts during the month of May, all with no reply. Yep, with both my hands slowly reaching into the air, I was that close to giving up, surrendering! A horrible bloody mess, and still worsening by the day!

I was glad I had informed Dr. Roberts that others, like Evelyn Thoms, also knew the way I felt about being let down, basically hung out to dry. Obviously, this had my mind spinning and had me considering anything which appeared to be a viable option. Whatever had been taking place in Roberts's professional or personal life, frankly did not involve us or belong in this arena. Again, I was frustrated beyond words.

At this point, it had been nine weeks. It had been nine long weeks since my last working day, and it was feeling much longer, being in this period of uncertainty. It was all much longer than I might have imagined. Regular therapy sessions carried on as I struggled to resist deeper depression due to the negative aspects of the past weeks.

I hadn't received any inquiries from Travis at work, but knew he deserved to be brought up to date with the situation. Through a text, I advised my claim presently remained on hold, as my case manager and the psychologist were still trying to contact each other. To verify such, I forwarded him a screen shot of the email I had received from Dr. Roberts, which sort of confirmed there were attempts being made.

Midway through the month of May '18, prior to working my final shift, my son Chris and I took off, driving southbound to Myrtle Beach SC, arriving the day after Randi, Marcel and the kids. We were set for a six-day mini vacation. Fun in the sun, beach and surf time, with my intentions of leaving all my worries back home in the driveway. The uncertainties which had been badgering me weren't welcome on this getaway.

Being the campers that my family are, they set up in a homey cabin at a local KOA while Chris and I checked into an ocean side cabin of our own at one of the Marriott's. We were located on the main strip, six floors up, which was to be our own style of roughing it for the next six days. With my history of back issues and quirky joints, I needed quality accommodations for the week and Chris didn't offer any argument.

Our lodgings were just minutes from each other so come morning, we would make our way to the campground where we all pitched in preparing breakfast and sipping coffees while the kids either rode their bikes or played nearby. I frequently initiated going for walks through the grounds where the kids were always eager to join in. With so much going on inside my head, I found being mobile in any form was a benefit and having the kids and one or more adults with me was a perfect distraction to ever so briefly push away the disorganized, troubling thoughts, thus replacing them with love, security, hope.

All things considered; I was still a walking disaster. Fragile and vulnerable, yet I was relieved to know the adults in my family hadn't picked up on any of it. Remember, PTDS sufferers are crafty at disguising the negative signs of our mental health to protect our loved ones from realizing the stresses going on within our affected minds.

All the 'what if's' from the past weeks continued to plague my mind, including the cold realization I had absolutely no control over any part of this. But for sure, being surrounded by family had removed part of the sting from my situation. We enjoyed full days lounging on the beach and playing with the kids in the surf, sightseeing on the piers while talking with anglers who had dropped their lines into the ocean twenty feet below the weathered boardwalks. Several of the fishermen were happy to talk and display their catch to the kids, who were just as willing to touch a few of them, including the baby sharks.

My grandkids, Tyler, Devon and Ava all enjoy the sport of fishing. Back home, when they get out on their mom and dad's pontoon boat for a day and manage to find a convenient place to drop their own lines, life just-gets-better! And, with three sets of grandparents who reside on the water, it makes for a perfect natural habitat.

On those mornings or afternoons when we decided we'd rather not fight the crazy crowds, hauling beach umbrellas, chairs, coolers and beach toys, we resigned to the heated pool within their campground where it was just as hot and sunny, the drinks were just as chilled and we usually had the pool (almost) to ourselves. The kids always had a blast no matter where we ended up. There was always plenty to see, whether we stayed on the grounds or ventured out onto the strip because the week we were down, it was bike week in Myrtle Beach, SC. There were dozens of motorcycles within the park where the kids had set up their cabin as home. The bikers we encountered were friendly, respectful and the kids thought their rides were pretty cool (as well as some of the wild characters who rode them). Ava, mind you, definitely wasn't a fan of the bikes with their loud, straight pipes. Too funny, said no toddler ever.

On our return from South Carolina, I had just two day shifts remaining. Several weeks earlier, I had spoken with my family of the difficult choice I had made, of stepping away from my role within EMS in order to focus on taking care of myself. It was no surprise they were in total support of my decision.

While performing as frontline paramedics, we tend to endless numbers of patients and their families who are usually in the midst of one of the worst days of their lives. Serious medical issues, chronic health problems, suicides, vehicle accidents, assaults. Suicides have taken place in almost every feasible area one could think of, and a few you likely haven't. One of those common areas is the basement in someone's home. We have been in more basements than we care to remember.

The Centre for Addiction and Mental Health is one of the world's leading research centres and is also Canada's largest mental health teaching hospital. A representative of CAMH called with a date of August 9th for my assessment and I was reminded I had been placed on a cancellation list. Once more, it spelled the gravity of my condition and I could almost feel my back being pressed against a wall in resistance. However, I also realized I needed to continue on while in search of any sort of a resolution.

Just because someone carries it well, doesn't mean it isn't heavy - our physical health is just as important as our mental well-being.

Throughout my career, I have made attempts to maintain a reasonable degree of fitness, all which played an important part for me in the performance of such a physically demanding occupation. That said, wouldn't it be interesting if I was able to have recognized the benefits I experienced mentally from engaging in the combination of both cardio and resistance training?

For several years prior to the onset of my symptoms, I participated in strengthening workouts as well as alternately running 5-10 kilometres, sometimes several days per week. I would like to think these activities delayed some of my symptoms or at least were partially responsible for being able to keep my head above the waters for many years. Studies have indicated that adults affected with PTSD who participate in a regular exercise regime (resistance training, weights, cardio) could notice a significant decrease in their symptoms and/or a delayed onset of them. There you go!

One of the tools I used frequently was a pull-up bar which was mounted on the low joists in my basement. The recent weeks had been disturbing enough at this period in my life, I questioned that maybe I needed a plan of sorts, to deal with the mounting mental anguish. Disappointment, lack of professional moral support and an unending sense of sadness continued as daily reminders of where I was and what I was up against.

When someone experiences a mental crisis, at some point they may try to reach out and contact a professional, someone in an authority position, hoping for security, assistance, guidance or simply a supportive hand. However, should they feel their psychological needs have not been taken seriously or their needs have not been taken care of, this could be a potential turning point in their crisis. It is vitally important that the one experiencing the crisis is made to feel undeniably supported. Depending on the quality and type of support made available to them, the direction of their personal crisis could feasibly swing either way; significantly better or decidedly worse.

One point which is crucial for anyone who is placed in charge of taking care of those in such a situation, is to be able to not just listen and hear what we are saying, but being able to listen, hear and truly understand what is being said.

Being face to face, one on one with someone has its advantages but what about my case worker, Evelyn Thoms? Does she get it? If she does, I feel she needs to put forth a different kind of effort to show a different, more approachable side of her. Some might throw out the argument that we aren't in a face to face setting, but that isn't always necessary to get the job done properly.

Individuals in an ambulance communication role extract information from callers and are able to obtain a clear message of what is happening from the heightened emotions and specific details obtained. Sometimes the message is clear, other times we need to dig a bit further. If we are able to obtain a decent read from this distressed caller in just a short phone call while under pressure, one would think that someone who is in the business of caring for others in a vastly different environment, might operate differently while in their role.

Case in point, and I'm sorry for the long-winded explanation: a number of years of my career was spent in an ambulance communications centre where we not only dispatch EMS crews and fire services to locations of various emergency calls, but we also maintain the role of a call taker. A call taker in a communications centre, whether it be in a police, fire or EMS environment, answers 911 lines from those requesting assistance with their own specific emergency.

Many of these callers are in an extreme emotional state while placing a call for someone who may be seriously ill or injured, or they are calling for help for themselves. Maintaining a role within a (emergency) communication's centre is a highly stressful occupation, and quite frankly, the only people who can relate to this level of intensity is someone who has actually been in that role, wearing the headset while sitting in that chair.

This may be a bit off topic, but those who are part of a 911 communications environment answering these calls have often been overlooked within the first responder ranks. They are, after all, one of the initial links within the 911 system and frequently receive less than deserved recognition. I would willingly slap down a hefty sum that the PTSD rate of these workers is considerably higher than estimated.

The individuals in an ambulance communications role also 'get it'. They are able to obtain a clear image of what is happening from the heightened emotions of the caller. If we are able to obtain a decent read from a distressed caller in just a short phone call while under these pressures, wouldn't it be realistic to think someone who is in the business of treating their clients in such a different environment, might possibly function differently while in their own role? There are several files of documents and reports sent to Evelyn Thoms from my therapist and much of the information contains very sensitive information which could depict a clear and obvious summary of a client (to someone in her position). I believe Evelyn Thoms has more than sufficient tools to conduct herself in a kind, empathetic fashion and I believe if she was figuratively pushed into a corner with this argument, she would dispute my version all while suggesting she has more than adequate character and qualifications to perform the necessary fundamentals in her role.

Sadly, I do not feel supported by this person and I don't think she gets it. And to someone in my precarious position, this is a very real concern. (We'll touch on this again a bit later).

CHAPTER SEVENTEEN

Coming almost full circle

As a sixteen-year-old kid, one of my summer jobs was that of a lifeguard and swim instructor at a nearby outdoor community swimming pool. I had obtained my certifications two or three years earlier and had been hired at age fourteen, by a different group of lifeguards. At the time, the age of fourteen was not exactly legal for the position it involved. However, we all know many things were conducted differently back then.

Our group of lifeguards was small, close-knit and efficient, and recognizing a child or an adult in trouble could almost be a daily occurrence. Our pool setup was not equipped with proper lighting for night swims which meant we needed to close up early.

One such evening, as the sun began its decent, we were ushering everyone out of the pool area after a busy and crowed family swim. While ensuring all families were exiting accordingly, I spotted a child in the pool, face down, not moving, about a foot beneath the water surface. As I ran across the concrete deck, I yelled to my partner Kelly before diving in towards the victim. I pulled him to the side of the pool, and while lifting him onto the deck I could notice his absence of breathing along with his blue face and lips.

On one end of the pool deck was a small shack, which by today's standards would have been a decent sized garden shed. Constructed of wood with the concrete floor, it contained all the necessities for a large pool: pool motor, filters, stored chemicals and various other equipment necessities. In the mid 1970's, having no such thing as a 911 system, we had written on the inside wall, next to the telephone, all the necessary seven-digit emergency phone numbers.

All my training relating to water rescue had begun four to six years earlier, and it began to kick in now. I began artificial rescue breathing (mouth to mouth) on this child of eight or nine and instructed my partner to call an ambulance. CPR techniques were still not part of rescue models especially within environments such as ours this evening.

Once Kelly returned, we switched roles. She took over the rescue breathing as I gathered towels to keep him warm. Not long after, our victim began vomiting and coughing. Kelly told me that after calling the ambulance, she had spoken with our supervisor to attend. While speaking with our boss, all Kelly needed to say was, "Bonnie, please come to the pool." The cracking and distress in Kelly's voice and the distant sound of the ambulance siren defined the entire scenario for her. By this time, the family swimmers had exited the pool, yet remained on the outside the fenced area as eager onlookers, yet no adult had come forward to claim this child.

This victim of near drowning was conscious and talking once the ambulance arrived, however, a near-drowning situation is still a very serious, potentially life-threatening circumstance. With still no sign of a responsible adult for this boy, the ambulance attendants departed for the Grey Point General emergency department. In time, we managed to track down the parent of this kid. However, instead of offering praise, she opened up on a tirade towards us for allowing her son to enter the pool setting on his own, during the family night swim. In our defense, we asked how were we to know which kid was accompanied by which parent. Obviously, this parent refused to own any responsibility of this incident. This was noted and when the boy attempted to enter during future family events, he was refused.

At the end of the day, how was I to know that in just eight years, I too would be wearing a similar uniform and responding in an ambulance myself? And ironically, I'd find myself working alongside of one of the guys who attended our pool call. (DD).

CHAPTER EIGHTEEN

Apparently, rock bottom has a basement.

Thoughts I was trying to make sense of continued to flood my mind. For years, I had been in a position of helping others and now, here I was, acting alone in my own struggle.

One of these thoughts had left me wondering. Who was to realize there would come a time when someone in a group of 'savers' would find themselves in a position in which they were the one who needed saving? As the phrase goes, "Who will be there to help the helpers?" and what quality of help will they receive in return?

Waking each morning with little to no sense of motivation can be a frightful, empty feeling. Everyday decisions demand attention: ensuring bill payments arrive on time, scheduled appointments are followed, family obligations are met and an array of other important responsibilities remain on track. As the days crept past, I found myself sleeping hours away mid-afternoon or other days, simply driving with no particular place to go, no destination in mind. I came to realize that I was slipping down further into my familiar darkness but strangely, with less will to find anyone to reach out to. I was becoming dangerously at ease with this disturbing mental state.

On a day nearing the end of July, I was anxiously pacing the room, considering whether I should make yet another call to Evelyn Thoms, with faint hopes of catching a strand of most anything worthy. Knowing how unwelcome my call would be, I placed it anyway. While speaking with Evelyn Thoms, I once again inquired if Dr. Roberts's vague letter would allow for any such chance of reconsidering my claim? Now, what just might be the definition of insanity? Asking the same question repeatedly, all while expecting or hoping for a different result. This was definitely my thought for the day.

Evelyn Thoms clearly wasn't in the mood. She was cold and merciless, which put me even more on edge and uncomfortable. In one of Dr. Roberts's latest emails, he was against sending me to CAMH, as the experience would exacerbate my symptoms. Again, I argued this point with Evelyn and I even mentioned Dr. Roberts was a specialist in psychological trauma, which was simply a ludicrous and reckless comment, stated on my behalf. He had submitted just one report this year, outlining my progresses and state of mind. I recall one of the last times I asked Evelyn Thoms if I was still required to attend CAMH and her response was simply, "If you want to get paid you do!" (Enough is enough G, as I try to convince myself).

While tears streamed down my cheeks, my voice crackled, becoming louder. I was now as loud as Evelyn, as she too, was yelling. She tried to have me understand by repeating something I had heard before; at that moment, it made literally no sense. "G, I haven't received any information to indicate your condition has even deteriorated." Nothing to indicate my condition had deteriorated . . . . Evelyn had the reports from Lorraine Wilson in her possession, yet she was unable to officially recognize the documents without Dr. Roberts' corroboration. I am infuriated with her statement but say nothing! Here I am, a client of WSIB and now on the doorstep of my own breaking point I am simply beside myself, having regressed, collapsed into such a critical period of mental anguish. Evelyn Thoms does not seem to recognize the devastating, grievous nature of my circumstance. Why hasn't she been able pick up on the signs? I was in a never-ending battle for my salvation, a battle which at this point, I know I have lost.

Over the previous days, I examined the consequences I could face had I been placed in such a desperate position, a position which has suddenly become a reality. Essentially, I have been denied a decision, a decision which, in my own heart and mind, should have been a clear, moral win once considering all the facts and notes. However, instead, I now faced a devastating result.

What more could this woman want from me? My primary therapist who knows me better than anyone, one who knows I am deeply affected, yet, to me, this woman on the phone remains a solid barrier standing between me and an accepted claim, which I believe I am entitled to. Not to mention, being denied would also bring about a financial setback which I wasn't ready to face.

At some point in our lives, we have all found ourselves in a financial struggle; as in a young family making a fresh start after one of them unexpectedly loses their job. Consider someone at retirement age who finds themselves in a struggle with a deteriorating mental health condition, who suddenly has an unexpected financial burden land in their lap. With irrational thoughts abounding, a general lack of confidence along with clouded judgment, we begin the inevitable collapse, erasing any sense of hope. Once again, I regrettably admit defeat!

It's the small things which most always make a difference. You are beyond worthy.

During a therapy session one year prior, I asked Lorraine Wilson why we have never discussed concerns regarding suicide. Generally, she answered, anyone who has come through her office door for treatment has considered or at least entertained the thought of ending their life. To suggest I had not contemplated these ideations would be an absolute, foolhardy falsehood.

For as long as I can remember throughout my career, I have been adamantly opposed to the thought of suicide. With years of experience dealing with the results of suicide, I was able to gain a firm understanding, one which allowed me to see and hear the desperation and to realize the circumstances with some of our patients.
These conditions are real to our patient and unimaginable to anyone else. There's a phrase which I have used for years that sums it all up nicely; suicide remains a permanent solution to a temporary

problem. Honestly, it won't come any clearer than those few words. There are those countless faces we see daily. On the street, in the grocery store, and on public transit are those who display no recognizable signs, none even visible to close family, friends or coworkers, that any hint of such an issue exists from within.

Those struggling don't always wish for their lives to end, what they want is their turmoil and unrest to cease and be eliminated.

CHAPTER NINETEEN

We have no idea the effect we may have on another.

A few years before the end of my career, we responded to a suicide attempt by a young teen who had communicated that a weapon was involved. It is common practice for paramedic crews to switch call for call, meaning taking turns being the driver, then you attend the next call. (Both can be equally enjoyable). I was up for this call, however, after weighing the circumstances, my partner Holly took charge of our patient. Once arriving at the emergency department, my partner shared that the trip into the hospital was pretty much uneventful, meaning there were no vast changes in the patient's condition.

Our patient had said next to nothing during the transport which was fine, as their nonverbal cues possibly indicated, *leave me alone, I have plenty of thoughts to process, much thinking to do*! To some, our patient may not have appeared to have been in an emergent condition yet, after addressing several factors prior to departing the scene and learning they had an established plan, we transported her as a high priority.

Entering into the emergency department, we were met by a number of other EMS crews who were also waiting to have their own patient assigned a room in the bustling department. Holly waited her turn to speak with the triage nurse while I stood alongside our patient in the crowed hallway.

The term triage refers to sorting, or the assignment of urgency. This is used regularly within EMS and hospitals when referring to a patient's condition and when triaging, it is determined who is most ill or injured among the patients seeking care. As paramedics, we could feasibly utilize this mental tool several times per shift. After Holly had explained our findings to the triage nurse and after considering many factors, the triage nurse also assigns the same

CTAS 2 priority; a high priority, just below the level of resuscitation. This is a serious event.

The emergency department has just so many treatment rooms and beds, so when ambulances continue to arrive on the department's doorstep with more patient's, a process within the ER will occur. Depending on the circumstances, the process may involve not only the charge nurse of the department but also a nurse manager and possibly others. Many patients already in a room within the department may likely consider their own specific condition to be among the highest of priorities, however, they are not able to view the bigger picture.

Everyone retains personal strengths, weaknesses and their own reasons why they need to deal with any set of circumstances, at any said time. Our patient was clearly attempting to deal with her own situation; she appeared calm, yet distracted. Maybe she also had no preconceived thought she would end up in an emergency department today, but here she waits. I initiated some chat which involved unrelated, insignificant events in her life and fortunately for me, she continued talking and welcomed my responses.

Paramedics have found themselves in countless situations having similar conversations and, depending on the situation, a structured criterion should be adhered while engaging very troubled patients, within their own, specific circumstances. Those starting out in an EMS position might experience a difficult time finding the appropriate words or remarks when addressing sensitive issues, whereas a paramedic with several years under their belt may be able to draw information from past experiences. We often find ourselves with someone who is looking for guidance and a sense of security, and I felt our patient was looking for some of their own recent troubles to be recognized.

Fortunately for me, she decided to open up. This young patient was clearly despondent and had attempted to reach out to friends and family, with no one able to interpret the signs she was exhibiting. Later in the day, someone she knew had spoken with a responsible adult and 911 was called.

Our patient said she felt alone with the feeling that her own opinions and present life situation weren't being taken seriously by others; this was something I could very much relate to. I allowed her to finish her unemotional statement before asking her if it would be alright for me to explain something quite relevant to her own situation, something which she might not be aware of.

The emergency department is a happening place at the best of times, today being no exception. We had been talking for the better of twenty minutes and that time had just sailed by with ongoing conversation and regular intervals of checking her vital signs. I believed I could offer some information which might benefit this troubled soul. Since I had her attention for the past minutes, I continued, not wanting for the opportunity to pass.

I asked her to look around at everyone in the department that she was able to see from our vantage point in the hallway and asked what she thought their roles could be. She answered there were two doctors (male and female), numerous nurses, also male and female, an X-ray technician, lab personnel, and various family members of in-house patients within the department along with four or five other paramedic crews.

I asked her to look around again and never mind what role they were in today. I watched her scanning the room, taking all this in. All of these people you see, I continued, have at least once in their lives felt similar to the way she was feeling today. Either at a young age or older, at one point they too had felt they were alone, unsure of themselves, was anyone really listening, and had questioned the direction their own lives were headed.

I added that some of the problems which we consider as permanent today, could actually turn out to be much different. Our room came available, we transferred our patient and updated the nurse responsible for her care. Holly and I said our goodbyes and I noticed a different look in this young girl's eyes, perhaps even a confident sparkle.

In my eyes, our patient had opened up, plenty! Hopefully she was able to carry on with the realization that she really wasn't alone that day, and she too, retained the powers within to adjust her own direction while she pondered her future. This was about good timing, which can sometimes play a major part in many of our life decisions. When departing the emergency department, Holly just shook her head, saying she couldn't believe that our patient had said nothing on our way to the hospital and then never stopped talking once there. I told Holly that our patient was the one who got me talking, and I just followed her lead.

I got lucky. I was able to place myself into the shoes of a teen struggling through such an awful period in her own life.

CHAPTER TWENTY

Here I sit in my living room, cell phone pressed to my ear, in conversation with Evelyn Thoms, again. Inside our homes, where everyone should experience a sense of security and peacefulness, immune from anything bad or threatening, I notice the love looking back at me as I admire the photos of my kids and grandkids. For reasons which I'm unaware, I feel I may have failed everyone, I've let them all down. I don't know when, why or how, only that I have!

Our voices in conversation continue on yet another phone call; a call which is subdued in comparison to the previous 'chat' which was heated and loud. Today's call began with an unusual theme. I explained to Evelyn Thoms I was apologizing for how I reacted on the phone, losing my cool, with a raised voice. Evelyn Thoms also professed she had allowed herself to lose her own self-control.

Again, I am desperate for anything optimistic to say or to hear from Evelyn. While Evelyn continued on her own soapbox, all I can think of are her own words from an earlier conversation, *'Dr. Roberts failed you!"* We close out the conversation with nothing memorable, leaving me with a strange, preoccupied stillness.

I stand and close the front door of my home. Looking about, I realize I simply have no argument left to offer the sharp voice to which I had been talking. This is nearing the end of July. Sixty-five days have passed since leaving work and my claim still remains unapproved, with no settlement in sight.

Sixty-five days could well be a drop in the bucket compared to the many others also awaiting positive news regarding their own claims, and perhaps their claim situations are far worse than mine, also due to unfortunate circumstances. My claim issue is different, regardless. It is considerably different because it is my own situation, and no one else's. It's mine. This was personal for me.

I haven't been negotiating with a panel to finalize details for a job competition, I am on the threshold of a life-altering decision. My mind then took me to a place I had not yet even considered: Evelyn Thoms was right, policy had not been properly followed. In my estimation, my claim could be denied as result of disregard for a patient's well-being. This wasn't my therapist who knows me inside out. It was Dr. Roberts who dropped the ball on this one. By the way, where is he, my registered psychologist? The one who had virtually abandoned me in such a desperate period of my life.

After the latest phone call with Evelyn Thoms had ended, I started yet another email to Dr. Roberts. Yup, once again I found myself explaining the latest status with WSIB, which had been placed in a ridiculous holding pattern. This claim of mine wasn't going anywhere.

As I sit here writing in my den, two plus years after that very phone call with Evelyn Thoms, documenting my thoughts that you're reading now, I wondered why had I placed so much emphasis on continually updating Dr. Roberts with details of all the negative events taking place between Evelyn Thoms, WSIB and myself.

What possible value could come out of rehashing these details? Reflecting on this subject, I'm certain many readers might also be asking the same question: why would I waste mental anguish, time and effort on someone who has demonstrated only vague interest in my own struggle? I figure this was the mettle I was made of, and it was my way of deciding, for the moment anyway, not to give up when everything around me was caving in.

I figure I had kept on hounding Evelyn Thoms for a couple reasons. She was accessible, she listened and I made her a verbal target of sorts, if nothing else. Who knows, maybe there was the slightest glimmer of a chance that she would alter her decision? But she answered her phone when I called, which gave me the opportunity to rattle her chain.

As far as Dr. Roberts was concerned, he remained inaccessible while I was coming apart, one strand at a time, desperate for anything positive. My tank was near dry, my gauge was reading zero. I wasn't up to even consider another approach.

As expected, the days following left me deflated and unable to react with any authentic emotion. Different endings continued to play out in my mind of the imminent disaster which I was facing. I asked myself if I was demonstrating the kind of thoughts someone experienced while going mad and becoming totally unglued. I felt I was gravely, morally injured. Then all the what if's began. What if, for some crazy reason, it was necessary for me to start back at day one with this entire situation, would I have the strength and be able to re-live the entire past ten weeks? I thought of that for a split second. Nope! Not a hope. But given my make up, it wasn't like me to just surrender, roll over and die.

We all know that Dr. Roberts had informed Evelyn Thoms that he objected to me being sent to CAMH, as it would send me backwards, possibly months, in treatment. But, what the hell did it matter at this point? The matter of it was, I hadn't considered one other possibility: what if the reps in Toronto didn't believe me? What if the information they gathered wasn't sufficient for them to arrive at a reasonable conclusion that my condition was genuine and I was legitimately suffering? What if, what if, what if! What if the damn sky wasn't blue anymore?! I couldn't take the chance having even one more negative blow. Just one more would be catastrophic, I was sure.

My date in Toronto was set for August 8th and 9th. I was to be housed for up to two nights, depending on the progression of the assessment, and the possibility of two days away from home wasn't sitting well with me. A day or so later someone else from yet another branch of WSIB called with another offer. If I wasn't up for the drive to Toronto, they would cover the cost for a seat on Via Rail. I would be travelling from Sterling Falls to Toronto. It's not like this was a trip through the mountains of western Canada. I told them I would drive myself, thanks just the same. I'm not usually the cynical type, but I felt the situation was warranted this day. If this tidbit of news was meant to brighten my day, it missed its mark by miles.

As for all the truly important people in my life, I wasn't even aware that I had been seeing less and less of my family than previous weeks. I was drawing myself away even more, once again.

CHAPTER TWENTY-ONE

Apparently, rock bottom has yet another level, even beneath its basement.

Even I was able to notice my binge drinking was becoming a very solid concern. I was a fan of cold beer and whiskey on ice and, over the past several months, the two were rarely not side by side on a table next to me; inside, outside, it didn't matter. This was occurring more frequently which no doubt contributed to increased episodes of depression, yet I was desperate to escape the feeling that all this claim crap would never be resolved in a positive light.

I would rarely drink in the afternoon and most days, I didn't have my liquid duos set up until after supper and seldom on consecutive nights, but lately, even my own bar hours were subject to change. On one of the last days of July, only a week or so before my scheduled date in Toronto, I found myself seated comfortably outside, on my open porch, enjoying the sights and sounds of a typical humid summer evening. My seating area for the evening is part of my eighty-year-old home. My porch is open and long and inviting to all. It's a perfect setting for me, along with assorted chairs and a 3-piece Bistro set.

Neighbours and other familiar men and women walking their dogs, or people just out and about might stop and chat, but not on this night. Perhaps I exuded an air of mystery or emotion which they took note of, and kept their distance. Maybe it was the sadness I exhibited, with slouched shoulders and my head no longer held high. The unusually loud and annoying vehicles were (strangely) barely an irritant to me this evening. My mind was focused on other matters. Matters of disturbing concern had been strangely welcomed inside my mind and had occupied front row seating, replacing all the 'what if's'. It appeared I wasn't going to be able to enjoy and soak in the beauty of this summer night.

I didn't know how but I knew that my life as I knew it then, would be changed upon my return from Toronto, bringing along the uncertainties of my future. Another thought had also occurred to me. Once my assessment was complete, Evelyn Thoms had explained the process included a one-month period, post assessment for WSIB to sift through the details to arrive at a decision. One month. Four weeks. Thirty days. Another eternity to wait...

When I asked, Evelyn Thoms informed me she retains a Bachelor of Sciences Degree, a BSc. I commended her with obtaining her degree and I wondered what, or if, supplementary courses are made mandatory or available to workers who are assigned the responsibility of working with clients within the Mental Stress Injuries Program? This position obviously includes some serious responsibility. Which clients of a case worker might happen to experience life altering and/or life-threatening consequences, once WSIB renders their decision? Are they all essentially deemed significantly altered? All, none, a handful? One would hope not all cases were this dire.

We might imagine these case workers to be part of enhanced programs, tailored specifically for the needs of such clients. For example: when I speak with my case worker, detailed notes are maintained, but are these notes/conversations shared with any higher-ups, or is the case worker working entirely independently? What if a concerning detail was overlooked or ignored? Should additional measures be implemented or considered upon realizing their client may well be in a period of serious crisis? Are other representatives of WSIB, specifically those holding psychological titles, being routinely informed or brought closer when the notes indicate something serious has come to light? It would not constitute a breach of confidentiality if policy was to indicate 'specific others be involved when necessary'. Why are personnel who retain the highest training or authority present, not granted direct involvement? This is a written rule in all frontline emergency agencies, hospital settings, and so many other businesses in general, why not in this case? Evelyn Thoms and I have had detailed conversations, one in which she mentioned in-house psychologists, however, there was no mention how much the psychologists became involved in case decisions. I had recently asked her directly about her background involving mental health clients. She answered that she did have the necessary training, but did not elaborate.

After the conversations in late July, I asked myself, where was Evelyn Thoms's integrity and professionalism, her own level of self-control and how did she allow herself to lose composure in such a sensitive situation? The records she maintains of our conversations and the various correspondence received from others related to my case should have had a dozen neon-coloured flags waving in her face. Could these have clearly indicated that I was someone in crisis? Yet nothing appeared to even acknowledge this fact. Maybe with enhanced programs, she might have recognized a red flag and responded differently. I feel, in the briefly detailed period I have known her, that she is lacking the skills to maneuver, seek out a solution and conduct herself professionally when in conflict with a client who has a heightened mental health condition. Maybe Evelyn Thoms did consult with others and share the information gathered. I have no idea.

There is a disturbing fact I learned while documenting my story. In conversation with a friend, they revealed that they have a relative who entered into a career with WSIB and once accepted, they attended the appropriate training. Apparently, they didn't have opportunity to enjoy a lengthy and fabulous career with this agency. The initial training subjects covered was none other than how to dispute or deny a client's claim. Wow! This person resigned, relating to their family that they would not have been able to live with themselves under such circumstances. Kudos to you, whoever you are.

Being my own bartender on this evening, I cracked open another beer and returned outside to the porch for just a few more minutes before heading inside, where I knew the humidity would be more bearable. Outside, I noticed the condensation forming quickly on the beer can. I wasn't able to get a clear head. I wasn't able to evict the torturous thoughts from my mind. They just refused to leave.

Once inside again, I noticed the sweat on my forehead and realized I was trembling but it wasn't from the cool temps of the A/C humming in the background. I began to weep as remembrances of a beautiful young person who had taken their life while at the end of their rope just months earlier. I wondered what had pushed them into the darkness, or what had drawn them into it. I set down my drink and stood up, having a destination in mind.

Without another thought, I walked through the room toward the back of my home and descended the stairs into the basement, where several times before, I had experienced these same dark thoughts. I already knew this role for which I had been cast, a role which I had rehearsed in a mental plan, but never took as far as I would come this night. The pull-up bar was mounted on the joists above my head, and I knew of its potential involvement in several disturbing thoughts. Everything was silent. I was totally alone.

As if on cue, I was suddenly jolted out of the frozen state I was in, with images of my family running through my mind. I became mindfully aware of what I had been considering. I glanced around then began sobbing. I stepped over a length of rope laying on the floor near my feet, before I ascended the stairs to the main floor. Upon entering my front room, I sat while experiencing a familiar emptiness.

As seasoned paramedics, we have witnessed (potentially) hundreds of post-suicide effects, and one of the most disturbing scenes remains the dreadful cries and wails from loved ones who had discovered the deceased or learned of their death. Such horrible sounds! Again, these memories were also safely secured.

My mind worked backwards to when I had thought of others, who, while forced into a similar circumstance, had to view their loved ones in such tragic, dreadful settings. I made a conscious vow to never, ever, place my family, my friends, my coworkers or anyone else in a similar hardship. Never! While in this grim period of my life, having visited so many dark places in my mind, I knew it was my family who had saved my life, having pulled me from this black and dismal event. They are all life savers, and they have no idea the scope of their actions today. I no longer needed to decide if I was going to live or die, I had already made that decision.

Soon after my one and only attempt to end my life, I had a clearer sense of where I was and which way I was headed. Through all the uncertainty and unfinished business, I was consciously aware I was no longer burrowing into the ground as before. I was changing my direction. I was definitely nowhere near out of the woods, but I knew I maintained a sense of control again, ever so slight but I was feeling something I hadn't experienced for some time. I was steering my own boat again.

CHAPTER TWENTY-TWO

Shameful realizations

Growth and a sense of renewed life come to mind. On my own, I had discovered the means to escape the darkest of the darkness, which, within seconds, could have cost my life, by my own hand. With shame, I admit that my temporary, personal moment of extreme selfishness and despair would have most certainly allowed a permanent and everlasting judgment for my beloved family. Not just family, but extended family, my friends, my co-workers and the thousands of fellow paramedics everywhere who work with courage and resilience, day after day, call after call.

With each person who takes their life, another 7-10 others will be deeply affected for years as the result. Let those numbers sink in. Because of the love of my family, I walked away from the point of no return. Not suicide. Not today.

What about the people suicide leaves behind? The survivors could have forever found themselves teetering on that invisible edge, resisting all what could have been drawing them towards their own clouded future. Suicide is not an answer. Family will never be better off without you. You will leave behind a void which can never be filled. NEVER! Reach out for help. If you can't do it for yourself, do this for the ones you love. Not Suicide. Not today.

CHAPTER TWENTY-THREE

Baby steps needed

This new-found life of mine was but the merest sliver of light which lit up between two rustic boards, just enough to allow the faintest stream of perceived sunshine on wherever was its intended path. To me, this was something new and polished, it meant volumes while dealing with my daily routines. The ground which I walked on felt more solid, but still, even the brightest days were still up for change.

The countdown was on for me to pack a bag and head into downtown Toronto. Bothersome thoughts would continue to plague my mind, anxieties were heightened. I would angrily lash out, reacting to some insignificant action, an inconsiderate driver or even my own annoyances would get the better of me. Nothing new here! Pretty much the only people I was able to behave and act normally around were my family and friends.

Once again, I was able to experience the comfort of frequent visits with my family and when talking with them about the upcoming assessment, I gave the impression that I would be attending a simple physical test, not some potentially life-altering psychiatric assessment. It was still all about protecting my family and there's no way I was going to open up and lay myself out to them. I knew Lorraine Wilson was worried about me; I could read some of her just as she could see right through me. Two days were set aside should this appointment require additional time. The day after those two days of assessment, I was scheduled back in Sterling Falls for an appointment with Lorraine Wilson, for a debriefing of sorts. We each knew whole heartedly I would need it.

CHAPTER TWENTY-FOUR

Every new day is a new challenge, a new focus, a new beginning.

Thursday morning arrived after a restless sleep, and I attended Lorraine Wilson's office at 10am for a neurofeedback session prior to hitting the highway for Toronto.

The best way to explain neurofeedback is this: for those affected with PTSD, the wiring in our head is in disarray, scattered. The neurofeedback process attempts to rewire the connection between the left and right sides of the brain, kind of like re-introducing them. Of course, this is a rather archaic explanation but the procedure is science-based and works well with EMDR treatments, as designed.

(When the Covid 19 pandemic initially hit and things shut down in March 2020, the in-office visits for neurofeedback were also cancelled as this is a procedure which cannot be done virtually. Treatments with EMDR sessions with Lorraine Wilson did continue virtually, and through our sessions, she had noticed the absence of neurofeedback was having a negative impact on my mental well-being. Once in-office visits were allowed again, neurofeedback sessions also restarted, until cancelled again a short time later).

I entered the highway early in the afternoon, genuinely looking forward to the drive. Not only had I driven forever throughout my career, but having been raised in Grey Point, we often made the trip to Toronto, Markham, Peterborough, Ottawa and beyond for various functions or to visit family. So, I wasn't intimidated by the volumes of traffic.

Considering what my mind was up against, I felt relaxed and my thought process remained clear, until switching onto the QEW from highway 403 at rush hour. Welcome to the gazillion lane racetrack which is peppered with drivers of every brand. I managed to slink into downtown TO, located the underground parking garage which, in my opinion, was designed more for European cars, not mid or full-size vehicles by any means. The concrete pillars displayed the paint, metal and glass evidence to verify just that.

While checking in to my hotel, I handed my documents to the young lady behind the desk who explained the various vouchers for meals, prepaid Beck Taxi transportation and instructions for pre-booking the transportation for the next day. I received my room card, headed to the 9th floor, then down a claustrophobic maze of hallways to my room. I'm not claustrophobic but imagined those who were, would not have had much fun navigating these hallways. And, of course, leave it to me, I imagined if there was ever a fire to break out in this high-rise with these narrow hallways, I'm certain we would all have perished.

Being comfortable, laid back and settled into my room was a comforting but distant thought as the familiar numbness had decidedly settled in next to me. I did try to look forward to participating as a wallflower in the restaurant on the ground floor, with a great view of the busy street just metres away. Something to drink and some chicken wings was all I needed on this hot August evening.

Who wouldn't want to sit and people watch in a bustling, unfamiliar area this evening? Note to self: the chickens in this area of down-town must have been of very restricted growth. I didn't spend long in the dining area before mindlessly heading upstairs. A quick chat in early evening with my son and daughter before drifting off into a medicated, uninterrupted sleep.

Once morning silently made its appearance, it would have been wonderful to have been able to have slowed my mind which was racing with unpleasant thoughts of the moral 'what if's'.

The breakfast dining atmosphere was nothing near as inviting as the night before. So unappealing! My stomach was rumbling but without an appetite, so I settled on a couple of beverages, including needed caffeine. I headed through the basement eating area toward the main lobby, distancing myself from the strangers who were still going about their own business at the buffet corral, and I imagined it was noticeable to others that I had a full docket on my mind.

The term hyper-vigilance refers to a state of increased alertness making you extremely sensitive to your surroundings, which has you always on your guard. Again, prior to becoming affected with PTSD, this alerted state was completely foreign to me.

While enjoying the sunshine on this beautiful morning, I thought it might have been obvious I didn't fit in while outside on the deep sidewalk, doing my best to maintain a calm demeanor while arranging for my taxi ride. Again, people watching is always an added bonus and a temporary distraction. The distinctive orange and green Beck Taxi arrived within minutes after calling and instinctively, I hopped into the front seat alongside the driver, a decision I soon regretted.

The driver was decently dressed and pleasant, but definitely not an award-winning conversationalist. A quick shoulder check into the back seat was looking more inviting, but too late for that! He requested my hotel information which corresponded to my identity and I asked about the travel time to CAMH. While avoiding eye contact, he answered ten to fifteen minutes. I asked, "Are you familiar with where to drop me off?" He answered, "Yes, we make this trip all the time." Ooooh, really?

My gut feeling suggested he seemed too nonchalant, and I should have known by his response that we, or rather I, was going to experience some kind of delay, which in turn would require me to double time it, so as not to be late! The driver pulls down into this empty ramp which resembles the old Victoria Hospital emergency department on South Street in London, minus the garbage dumpster on the right. I ask, "Are you sure this is the right place for a drop-off"?" But then again, who was I to question him? He assured it was the place so off I headed to the glass doors at the bottom of the ramp.

As soon as I entered the building, I knew I was in the wrong place, and the sole person in the area was a bored looking security guard who was seated on a chair inside the doors. Geez, I knew I should have asked him to wait! I checked over my shoulder and the cab was already out of sight. Man, he must have backed up and out of that ramp and zoomed off pretty darn quick! There was no sign of anyone else, medical or otherwise, inside the area as one might expect. Here we go!

"You can't get there from here," the guard says. Of course, I can't! Good thing I hadn't tipped that driver! The soft-spoken security guard provided me with some less than straightforward, 'there from here' directions to the appropriate entrance, which happened to be on the opposite side of the building. Guessing I'm up for a bit of a hike. "You can't get there from here", still made me laugh.

CHAPTER TWENTY-FIVE

Down to business

My plan originally had me arriving twenty minutes early to allow for such incidents, so I was relieved when I eventually found my way to the right floor and met up with a genuine receptionist, with minutes to spare. I was escorted to a waiting area just steps away where I completed the necessary paperwork then awaited my call.

A few minutes had passed when I was approached by a young woman who introduced herself as one of the psychologists. She appeared young for her role in this setting. I guessed her to be in her twenties and after exchanging pleasantries, she escorted me down a wide maze of hallways into a small office which was attached to another office. This maze of hallways seemed strikingly familiar and brought me back to a number of other, similarly designed facilities like St. Thomas, London, Grey Point and now Toronto.

Another woman joined us soon after, and introduced herself as a psychiatrist. Both women individually explained how things were going to proceed this morning and due to a scheduling issue, they would both be sitting in this morning to direct this assessment. The scheduling issue suited me just fine. They also advised that the assessment would take several hours and depending on their progress and findings, it could be extended to include the next day.

Considering the circumstances, both women had me feeling relaxed, safe and welcomed, however, I knew in my own mind that those feelings could change in an instant. Regardless, my feelings with these two professionals gave me confidence and they encouraged me to believe this was another step forward.

These were two no-nonsense ladies who got right down to business. From the beginning, they established the assessment I was about to undertake was voluntary and did not constitute a treatment model per se. Confidentiality, as laid out by the College of Psychologists and Physicians/Surgeons was explained and it was indicated that no impairment in my ability to provide consent was perceived, and verbal and written consent were provided prior to proceeding with the assessment.

In fairness to all of you, I won't dive into each and every topic addressed that day but I will cover a necessary handful. Pretty much every part of my life was covered at some point during the assessment, from present day then rewinding to my life growing up from a young age with my brothers and both parents. We had a good life which included an early introduction to hockey and competitive swimming throughout Ontario, followed with various high school sport activities. They ruled out any learning disorders during my education and noted that I experienced a brief period where I was bullied in elementary school, which proved difficult for me while I was younger. This circumstance took a positive turn when I taught myself how to navigate through difficult periods and found I was more than able to take care of myself in other ways.

The years of our marriage, our life, and the birth of our children was found to be a happy period. Going forward from there indicated a time when I independently attempted to understand why I was feeling the way I had been, having invested near twenty years in my field when I began to distance myself from my family.

The period of my employment beginning in 1982 was reviewed, which included a grim period involving multiple pediatric deaths within 8-10 years of the beginning my career. Then, fast forward to the summer of 2018 after I left my career. This part of the morning included the period of mounting hope and frustration that my psychologist, Dr. Roberts, would reconnect with representatives of WSIB and submit his updated progress reports as requested.
We spoke of my immediate family and their positive role as part of my own support network, and the inclusion of coping strategies

used for various situations. Workplace injuries and substance abuse was discussed. My participation with substance abuse was identified as a maladaptive coping mechanism and the history of ongoing workplace injuries was also noted.

Past EMS (notable) experiences, identified anxieties and hyper-vigilance symptoms which exist presently within my personal life were also discussed. Several examples refer to the safety of my grandkids and various activities which involve them on any given day, which can enhance these symptoms. (ie: past incidents involving swimming pools and associated safety measures, eating specific foods which reference children/adults choking, passenger safety within a personal vehicle, to mention a few). These examples may sound insignificant and possibly strange to some, but they are very real and can present disturbing results to those who are affected.

Here is one example which was documented that day: My granddaughter was eighteen months old or so when I would sometimes pick her up from daycare and take her home. We would usually chit chat all the way back to her house, however, if she was to go into an extended period of no talking/chatter, I would need to pull the car over and check that that she was in fact conscious and breathing. To my relief I would open the rear door and there she'd be, secured safely in her rear facing seat, smiling ear to ear, clearly occupied with whatever else. Remember, for those with PTSD, it's not about what might happen, it's about what actually did happen that we were a part of. It's about remembering. Sometimes it's not always a mentally 'sunshine and rainbows' period while experiencing these situations.

The two doctors and their interview subject were on a roll, cruising through the morning hours, mutually agreeing to carry on, and not stopping for a break until lunch. I still wasn't interested in eating but knew it was in my best interest to do as I hadn't since the night before. Up until now through the assessment, all I'd had was water and fruit juices. Everywhere was crowded, so I settled on a familiar fast food place and scarfed down something quick. I returned to the room I had left about forty minutes earlier and the doctors were already present, possibly eager to get down to the afternoon business.

When things began that morning, I was being interviewed by the psychologist while the psychiatrist was softly clicking away nearby, recording everything on a laptop, looking up and commenting periodically. That afternoon, their roles switched and the psychiatrist began with her questions. Things progressed as the mornings' timetable did, with questions involving several different topics and once again, we mutually agreed to defer breaking to continue until their questioning was complete.

Come mid-afternoon I sensed that things might be nearing their conclusion, what did that mean? Was the afternoon coming to an end so early? Were we finishing up after such an exhausting day? This couldn't be further from the truth.

What followed was a written assignment of approximately 300 questions. My responses on the assignment might assist in confirming or the diagnosing of several mental health issues, all dependent on how the blocks of questions, broken up through the pages, were answered. Additionally, the design of the test questions might ensure manipulation of the analysis would be that much more difficult.

If I considered the earlier session of verbal questioning to be taxing, the written segment of the day was brutal in its own way. The two women managing today's assessment seem to run pretty much nonstop and once the attending psychiatrist's role finished just prior to the written portion, she wished me all the best and excused herself as she was onto her next assignment.
Several times I've brought up the 'moral injury' element which, without any doubt, has been my primary concern. At the end of the

day, the conclusion of the assessment, the attending psychologist provided a summary of their findings, saving the best for last: it was on their recommendation to WSIB, "that I was not to return to my field of EMS in any capacity", and, there should be no difficulty in having my claim approved. The final say remained with WSIB, yet all appeared positive.

The above paragraphs, my Coles notes version of this day, explaining the details of my assessment, illustrate the vastness of topics addressed and questions presented in just over eight hours. And *no, you can't get there from here* still bounced around in my head.

On completion of the day at CAMH, the psychologist asked if I was okay finding my way out and directed me to the elevators. My orange and green taxi came to a stop curbside where I hopped into the back seat, which meant, leave me alone, I have thinking to do! The ride back to the hotel was uneventful and after gathering my things upstairs in the fire trap wing, I joined others in a meandering lineup, awaiting our turn to check out. While in line, as if on cue, my daughter and son called back to back, inquiring on the day and when was I coming home to Sterling Falls. These few minutes chatter with each of them was beautiful music to my ears, exactly what I needed.

Heading for an elevator which would take me down to the parking level, who do I run into? I meet a coworker visiting the city with his family. We make small talk where I tell them that I, too, am with family and heading home. No misrepresentation there, my family was with me, within my chest. I locate my car and after quick inspection, I determine it's just the way I left it the afternoon before, with no missing paint or new dents. (Might have been a bonus parking next to a cement pillar).

I'm now on my way out of the city, and being a Thursday, it was a typical day in the jungle. It wasn't rush hour on a Friday afternoon, I had spoken with my kids, I'm on my way home, traffic isn't bad and I'm listening to the tunes on XM radio.

I notice things change gradually around the Hamilton/Grimsby area on the QEW. Not with the traffic, but with me. I was becoming fidgety and nervous. I knew, and everyone involved knew from Dr. Roberts's earlier warning, that this assessment would come at a cost.

Depending on the subjects covered after a treatment session with Ms. Wilson, later same day or the day following, I could be thrown into a funk, a type of numbness and silence, to which I am accustomed. Rehashing events for purposes of treatment will do this and the events of this particular day were no different. But still, it was considerably different. This was more than having worked through a single session. Today's events at CAMH had opened a box, a box I wasn't familiar with, but I was no doubt becoming introduced to while seated in the fast food restaurant just off the QEW. The post-effects of the assessment did in fact last about 5-6 weeks before noticing I was back on track. Increasing EMDR sessions and neurofeedback sittings were two treatments which helped restore my health after my time in Toronto.

During the past 8-9 hours that day, once I started talking, I hadn't stopped. Aside from introductions of my family background, living within my family unit and like developments within the theme, several of the remaining topics included details which were troubling and very disturbing. It was these recollections, pulled out of my vault, which would exacerbate my condition. While in the restaurant I remember receiving a text from a friend who was checking up on me post-assessment. In my reply, I explained what I was feeling. They also knew of the debilitating symptoms brought on by the treatments and offered to drive down and pick me up, I assured them I was alright to finish the drive home and I'd message once arrived. I knew I was OK; I'd been in this situation dozens of times.

So, I shrugged it off, picked up my coffee and set out for the highway again. This time the tunes were loud and hard for most of the way home, just the way I like it! Music is one of the most enjoyable distractions for me and I find it redirects my focus from uncomfortable thought processes to a laid back and calm atmosphere. It's been a sort of refuge for me, for decades! And, even with these invading thoughts, I can assure you, I've always been safe while behind the wheel.

Our minds can be a wonder of science, and they can also be quite confusing to understand. During this assessment, possibly out of shame or fear, I did not disclose my suicide attempt just one week earlier. Soon after the assessment however, all persons and agencies which provide me with treatment had been appraised of the incident. Through local treatment after my assessment, Lorraine Wilson was also aware of my actions on that evening. She already had a clear idea about it, all without me telling her directly. She does know me inside-out and later took time to explain that I hadn't disclosed the incident outright, simply because 'I' wasn't ready mentally to open up.

CHAPTER TWENTY-SIX

You might never understand, until it happens to you.

One month after my assessment, I headed north on highway 400 toward the Muskoka's to meet up with my daughter's family in the Port Carling area, where they had rented a lakefront cottage for the week. Lake Rosseau was the beautiful view offered from the lakeside rooms of their cottage, which was built high up on the rocks. The temperatures were cool during the week in early September 2018, but there was nonstop fun. There were walks through the forest on the cottage roads where naturally, every kid would inevitably zero in their own walking stick (or sticks), exploring in the woods, afternoon and evening bonfires, BBQs, fishing for the kids, and canoeing.

One afternoon, after the rain had cleared, with just a light wind remaining, Marcel and I took the boys for a canoe ride into part of the lake across from our cottage toward a large island. The island had a number of large cottages/homes scattered about, so we headed in that direction to take in the view.

As you know, I have been around water activities for most of my life and had never experienced any negative mental issues while around it, until now! About 15-20 minutes into the crossing, we were better than half way when my mind simply took over and allowed the darkness inside. And once again, along came a string of the what ifs. What if we were to capsize this far out, what would happen next? I hadn't considered it until much later but with all the cottages in the area and people out and about, in front and behind us, someone would have certainly taken note and assisted. That said, the water conditions were not rough and posed no threat. Throughout several of my water safety programs I even had the know-how to right the canoe and have it empty of all the water, even in the depths of a lake. We would have been wet and cold, but otherwise, we would have been fine.

I had been taken back to another time, reminded of several ambulance calls I had attended, with some being decades back. Events which didn't end well. I held onto the idea of forging ahead, all while trying to rationalize the thoughts, until I was eventually overcome and knew we needed to cancel this outing and turn back. Marcel was paddling in front and once I mentioned what we needed to do, I could feel his sense of disappointment, observing his shoulders drop. I muttered something to the boys something I knew they'd understand, along the lines of needing to go to the bathroom.

While pulling alongside the dock, my granddaughter was excited to see her crew who had made it back, however my daughter had a puzzled look of wondering why we had turned around. After the two kids explained to their mother that "grandpa had to poop", once they were safely out of earshot, I spelled out the actual reasoning. I had experienced a nasty episode of true anxiety. I'm thinking this was the first time they were witness to such an event, an event I had wrestled with many, many times in the past. I was quite disappointed in myself for having being responsible for taking away their water adventure for the afternoon. To my relief, Marcel set out again later, this time on his own and was able to take in the scenery which we had all been waiting to catch a glimpse of.

When I was invited to come north with family, I believed the time away would be a positive time to share, especially having it be one-month post assessment. Today, I look back on this as being one more opportunity to accept things as they are and how they present on any given day. PTSD factors can and will show up any time they damn well please. I am sorry my episode changed our canoeing plans of the day, yet I would rather our plans were changed than to never have had the opportunity to enjoy the setting of those four days together. I live with PTSD, and life goes on!

CHAPTER TWENTY-SEVEN

If you're through learning, you're through.

Life, in fact, did carry on. My WSIB claim was approved, and they repaid my employer monies owed since my employer had fronted the money prior to my claim being approved. Months since leaving work have slowly turned to a few years. I still maintain close contact with friends and co-worker friends, but I knew I was now part of the inevitable 'drifting away syndrome', drifting away from the whole thirty some odd years in this field. Pre-Covid, we enjoyed our coffee/porch visits, two-hour riverside talks and lunches out at our favourite locations, but even Covid wasn't able to cancel messages, phone calls and drive-by speed chats by a few ambulance buddies.

Today, being part of the outside-looking-in crowd, the positive memories I hold have an even greater meaning and will have for years to come. It's all a different show now. Back in the day, when taking the time to recall certain events, events where you know that you and your partner's efforts clearly made a difference in the outcome of someone's life, those recollections might not have felt all that distant. It didn't matter how long ago they happened, they still felt fresh and recent. After all, still being on the job, wearing the uniform, who knows if these or similar events might just happen again?

While recalling similar circumstances where we had made a difference; these don't feel as recent and as fresh today. Now, over two years later and me on the outside of the glass, the memories, once very real and unblemished, feel distant, maybe even blurry. I know there won't ever be a 'might just happen again' moment. I want to learn how to hold onto such special periods and I wish all of my positive memories to remain just as clear and bright as the day they happened.

November 2020: Two and a half years after my visit to Toronto, I was again present for my second assessment with CAMH, this time facing my laptop in my own home. We spent a few hours going over several topics and one of their recommendations was for me to attend the Bellwood Treatment Centre in Toronto where I would receive therapy for addiction and treatment for PTSD. Once they mentioned my attendance was required for a period of eight weeks, that changed everything. I flat out told them this would not be possible and I explained why.

I recognize my family, all six of them, as my established support network and without them, I knew that being away for those fifty-six days would be detrimental to my well-being. I could fully appreciate the intentions of the psychiatrist and psychologist in addressing my alcohol habits but I still declined. None of their recommendations were an absolute requirement to be put into play; they were strong, well-intended suggestions considered from their own professional positions, designed to provide well-meaning treatments, guidance and direction.

I was well aware my alcohol habits were clearly not a benefit for my mental health treatments and there were several times where I had taken a step back while seriously considering my evening routines. Sitting in my home one evening while on the laptop with my usual liquid duos next to me, it came to mind that I didn't and wasn't receiving any genuine pleasure sipping the beer and whiskeys on ice as much as I once had. They were there as my own (mostly daily) medicinal treatments used to activate a 'comfortably numb' sensation as I've talked about earlier. (Pink Floyd right now)?

(Earlier on I had referenced undergoing knee surgery. This is similar, but in a different context). I had entered Sterling Falls Health Alliance, my local hospital, in September 2019 where I underwent a total knee replacement and once home, I ceased taking alcohol all together for thirty days. I knew it would be counterproductive to combine the prescribed post-surgery medications with booze and had no problem removing it from my daily ritual. More importantly, aside from the alcohol and medication combinations, I was also concerned with potentially experiencing an episode where I'd lose my balance, 'and experience a holy whoops', whether on dry flooring or in the shower. And specifically, while showering, the last people I wanted to welcome into my bathroom to lend a hand were any of my EMS buddies. Well, I guess I can think of a few I might! Lol!

Less than two weeks after my second CAMH assessment, I made an important decision. Over the years, I had initiated a hold on consuming alcohol only a handful of times, with nothing overly serious, as the only person I shared any responsibility to was myself. Realizing the numerous benefits of abstaining I decided that evening to take this one step further and involve more than just myself. I sent a lengthy message to my son, my daughter and my son-in-law outlining my intention. Now I was responsible to my family, too!

After sending the message to my family, I decided that it was time for action. That evening, I stopped taking alcohol on all accounts. I had learned of several advantages of not including alcohol in your daily life and now I was able to experience them personally. A clear head, better sleep, gradual weight loss and I was also receiving comments that my skin and eyes looked clearer. The bonus was that some of these comments were from people who had no idea I was no longer drinking.

Sometime earlier, even prior to my November assessment, I visited the CAMH website. I was looking for information which would help identify whether I had a substance abuse problem, an addiction problem, or both. Through the information that the website provided, it suggested I was living with a substance abuse issue. Through this probing I also found CAMH had developed an app, 'Saying When'. This is a researched program which aims to help people understand and control their alcohol consumption. It shows people how to track drinks and their urges to drink, how to set goals and show progresses. Entering my seventh month of abstinence as I write this, I feel I am well on my way to a new me!

Early in 2021, I made a detour and pulled up alongside a few EMS crews who were preparing to depart the ambulance bay or had just arrived. I was able to speak briefly with a handful of my friends and after each and every spontaneous quick chat, I came away from it with a feeling of elation. As you all know and have read so many times already, I so loved this job. I have the utmost respect and admiration of all our men and women everywhere who remain part of this challenging field.

One of my friends that afternoon had offered some very comforting and encouraging thoughts of his own and even later, added more via message which I received 4-5 hours after our afternoon meet up. Not everyone I worked with had knowledge of my story of PTSD, or even the reason I remained off work. Many had suspected I was away due to my long history of back issues; others figured I had silently slipped away and retired. This one friend who I will call Marvin, was aware of many of the facts, even prior to this work being published. Therefore, it's safe for me to say I am reasonably open with others regarding my journey, which may depend on the type of relationship I have with these people. So, depending on your own friendship with Marvin, he is a man who will always have your back and always, 'tells it like it is'. Marvin wanted me to know that my struggling openly has had a positive impact on him and he is sure it has affected others, too. His comment afforded me such a reassuring foothold, mainly because that was one of my primary ambitions for writing. He went on to say, "You bring me hope G, and a lot of us are going to need to deal with some version of what you are struggling with, and to see you working towards healing makes me (Marvin) feel much safer and, that there is a path forward."

He went on to say that my progress, "denotes me as a target for the rest of us to beat". "You bring me hope", he said! "Keep struggling".

This comment was such a breath of fresh air, to know there are others throughout our own emergency services who can undeniably recognize ongoing or potential concerns within themselves, being affected by many of the same struggles I still face. This is such an important first step to be recognized, when something just doesn't feel right anymore. I am not suggesting I am happy they were struggling too, but they were recognizing their struggles and becoming aware that they may need assistance.

Parting thoughts

In the words of Alex Trebek: "I'm able to perform and handle the show (my job) because I like it. It's a good job, everybody out there should be able to have this kind of job. It is something you enjoy doing, something you're proud of doing and something that pleases (helps) people and pays you a pretty decent salary." These were my thoughts about my job as well.

When I entered the ambulance course in 1981, I had no earthly idea that my career would take me to the vast array of places and situations I would experience, to visit the thousands of wonderful people I have met. There have been those who have asked, had I had my magical crystal ball with me that day in 1981, and had the opportunity to view nearly four decades ahead, what might the results have shown? Would I have remained on a course heading of where I am today or considered something which held less emotional exhaustion? Would I have seen all the exhilaration, fright, shock, chaos, side-splitting laughter, heart-wrenching loss, horror, camaraderie and everlasting friendships, unfathomable devastation, and the blessings of newborn lives? In all probability, yes, all while shaking my head with uncertainty. In the end, after heartfelt reflecting, I am truly happy I didn't have the crystal ball that day.

I want to point out, that if you suffer with mental health issues or PTSD, there is help out there, and you are worth the time and effort invested to find the suitable pathway for you. Remember, healing takes time. Be patient with yourself! I was never a 'pill guy' up until 4 years ago, and now I have my own arsenal of medications which help to keep me between the lines, and my health is better for it. With my PTSD, my treatment may be ongoing for life. That being said, I completed my third assessment with CAMH in February 2021.

I am left with a feeling of being blessed where I am in my life. Many of the roads on my journey have been altered in various ways, where things have turned out differently than I thought they would, or things have gone very wrong. Yet, here I am, exactly where I choose to be.

One day, you will all be retired. You will still retain the smarts and sensibility regarding your work like it was yesterday, reciting protocols and whatever else occupies your mind at the time while reminiscing. You will reach that period in your life before you know it; I was there once and here I am today. Time passes us by too quickly my friends. As it's been said and suggested more times than we can remember: please make added effort to slow yourself down, enjoy the beauty around us and don't forget to smell the fragrances of life.

I exhort you to be safe and take care of one other. Hug, snuggle and love those little ones.

G. F Connors

gconnors08@hotmail.com